OF HUMAN FREEDOM

JEAN-PAUL SARTRE

Of
Human
Freedom

Edited by Wade Baskin

PHILOSOPHICAL LIBRARY
New York

FOREWORD

Webster's *New Collegiate Dictionary* defines existentialism as "an introspective humanism or theory of man which
expresses the individual's intense awareness of his contingency [that is, the brute fact that he happens to exist in a
situation and has the possibility of shaping his own life] and
freedom." This definition, though framed with a view to
encompassing divergent trends in contemporary thought,
calls attention to the salient features of the philosophy of
the most influential writer of our time. Jean-Paul Sartre's
concept of anguish subsumes man's intense awareness of his
contingency and freedom: man enters a totally meaningless
world, makes it habitable through his consciousness, confers
meaning on it through his free choice, and is overawed by
the dreadful freedom which makes him responsible for his
situation and his life. Anguish that results from man's recognition of his existential situation, man's inhumanity to man,
man's search for social justice—these are pervasive themes
in Sartre's works. The following selections, arranged chrono-
logically according to the date of their publication in French,
are intended to reflect the range and diversity of his thinking
on those issues which directly affect the freedom and the
rights of man. They span two decades and provide insights
into the evolution of his thought through diverse stages—
from the resolution of the existential crisis through art (in
Nausea) to the reconciliation of existentialism and Marxism, the discovery of personal meaning and values through
the social function (in *Search for a Method*).

Nausea (1938) advances themes that have since become commonplace: Nothingness, the absurdity of life, man's solitude and alienation, man's confrontation with anguish and despair. "When Sartre, the philosopher, informs us that we have an immediate intuition of existence in the sensations of boredom and nausea, we tend to raise an eyebrow," Germaine Brée and Margaret Guiton wrote in *An Age of Fiction* (1957). "But when Sartre, the novelist, describes this situation, we are almost convinced."

The power of Sartre's fiction lies in the clarity of his images and the universality of the truths which he exposes. *Nausea,* a landmark in existentialist fiction, is generally recognized as his most significant novel. Its "hero," Antoine Roquentin, is a writer who meticulously records his impressions of people and objects in the world with which he attempts to come to terms. Roquentin's struggle provides Sartre with an opportunity to dramatize his discovery of "the key to existence, the key to my Nausea, to my own life." The traditional means for escaping from Nausea—rational humanism, civic enterprises, travel, adventure, scholarly research, human love—are found wanting. The metaphysical anguish which he experiences as a result of his confrontation with the chestnut tree—now a familiar image in literary criticism—is the turning point in his life, for in the loathsome void of his own existence he glimpses the possibility of creating his own essence and perpetuating his own freedom. Like Hamlet, Don Quixote, and Holden Caulfield, Antoine Roquentin has become an archetype. His plight is the plight of modern man, who must re-establish the meaning of human freedom in an irrational world.

The philosophical basis for the existentialist conception of human freedom was laid in *The Psychology of Imagination* (1940). Here Sartre examines the function of consciousness in creating a world of unrealities, probes the nature of the psychic life and the mind's complex ties with the outer world, defines the intentional structure of the image and the uniqueness of man's freedom to create, and concludes that "the imagination is the necessary condition for the freedom of empirical man in the midst of the world."

The first full exposition of the doctrine of freedom is in the monumental but difficult *Being and Nothingness* (1943), which established Sartre's reputation as the leader of the philosophical movement generally associated with his name today, and which brilliantly illustrates the dictum of William James: any new theory goes through three "classic stages"— first it "is attacked as absurd; then it is admitted to be true, but obvious and insignificant; finally it is seen to be so important that its adversaries claim that they themselves discovered it." The existential situation—man's anguish, his aloneness, his dreadful freedom—dominates much of recent literature; its influence is traced through the writings of Sartre's predecessors and successors; its reality is felt by serious thinkers everywhere.

In the section of *Being and Nothingness* excerpted here, Sartre shows that the freedom of man cannot be separated from the being of man, that human freedom precedes human existence and makes it possible, that consciousness of freedom means consciousness of our own possibilities, that freedom is the basis for all human activity, and that responsibility "is simply the logical requirement of the consequences of our freedom."

That the writer must concern himself with contemporary problems and issues—must use his own freedom to promote the freedom of all men—is implicit in most of Sartre's writings. In *Anti-Semite and Jew* (1946) he examines, objectively, a problem rooted in the existential situation. His logical exposition leads to the inescapable conclusion that an abridgement of the rights of one man is the enslavement of all men, that "not one Frenchman will be secure so long as a single Jew can fear for his life."

Antoine Roquentin's decision to turn to writing as a possible solution to the existential problem may have been the prelude to a theory of aesthetics adumbrated in *What Is Literature* (1948), the volume in which "Why Does One Write?" was first published. In his classic literary manifesto, Sartre defends the right of the artist to be committed to a cause. He answers those who charge him with attempting to murder literature by calling attention to their confusion—since they have never defined what writing is, why men write, or for whom men write—and by showing that the writer has not only the freedom but also the obligation to become involved in contemporary issues. He concludes that "the freedom of writing implies the freedom of the citizen," and that "writing is a certain way of wanting freedom."

Saint Genet (1952) might be subtitled "Freedom to Do Evil." Jean Genet, the subject of Sartre's passionately devoted treatise, is known in the United States chiefly for *The Blacks* and *The Balcony*—two disturbing plays that project on the stage perversity, brutality, and evil. Genet's life provided him with the raw materials for his plays and novels. Born a foundling, he spent the first thirty years of his life in reformatories, prisons, and the haunts of criminals. He decided to be what he was said to be and, free of guilt feelings, to live a life of crime and debauchery. Sartre lauds him for choosing the existence of thief, traitor, pervert, and pornographer. The world of brutality and betrayal recreated in his works provides Sartre with the springboard for a new assault on those who would suppress human freedom, for to him Evil is a myth which "right-thinking" people have developed "by depriving human freedom of its positive power and reducing it to its negativity alone."

Albert Memmi, the author of *The Colonizer and the*

Colonized (1957), was born in Tunis, where he had ample opportunities during his childhood to observe the effects of oppression and persecution in the colonial situation. In his "Introduction" to Memmi's essay, Sartre expresses his deep-seated sympathy for all those who are forced to endure injustice. He shows that "colonialism denies human rights to human beings" and keeps them in a subhuman condition, and he sees in this system the mechanism of all oppressions of one individual or group by another, in every part of the world.

Search for a Method (1957), the work from which the final selection is taken, was written as a partial answer to critics of *Being and Nothingness* who complained that there was no room in his philosophy for any positive social theory. How can the individual cultivate his own freedom and at the same time contribute to the society to which he belongs? The answer to this crucial question is fully elaborated in *Critique of Dialectical Reason,* a work still not available in English. *Search for a Method* is a useful summary of the larger work, in which he analyzes man's relation to the group, the nation, history, and the universe. Written originally for a Polish magazine (it was revised and reprinted in *Les Temps Modernes*—the journal founded by Sartre—under the title "Existentialism and Marxism" and as the prefatory essay in the first volume of the *Critique*), it represents the author's most recent attempt to provide a philosophical system to bridge the gap between Marxist and non-Marxist thought. In the concluding part of the essay he expresses the hope that Marxist thought will take on "the human dimension (that is, the existential project)" and will become "the foundation of all inquiry." Thus he looks toward the foundation of a social order in which the full implications of man's unique freedom will be realized.

Southeastern State College   Wade Baskin

CONTENTS

Foreword   v

The Meaning of Existence: *Nausea*   1

Freedom to Create: *The Psychology of Imagination*   7
    1. Consciousness and Imagination   7
    2. The Work of Art   22

Freedom to Have, to Do, to Be: *Being and Nothingness*   32
    1. Freedom: The First Condition of Action   32
    2. Freedom and Facticity: The Situation   56
    3. Freedom and Responsibility ✓   93

Freedom from Persecution: *Anti-Semite and Jew*   99

Freedom to Write: *Why Does One Write?*   105

Freedom to Do Evil: *Saint Genet*   129

Freedom from Exploitation:
The Colonizer and the Colonized   137

A New Approach to the Philosophy of History:
Search for a Method   144

Bibliography   150

xi

ACKNOWLEDGMENTS

"Nausea," translated from *La Nausée* by Lloyd Alexander, 1959. Copyright © 1964 by New Directions Publishing Corporation.

"The Psychology of Imagination," translated from *L'Imaginaire, psychologie phénoménologique de l'imagination,* 1940.

"Being and Nothingness," translated from *L'Etre et le Néant* by Hazel E. Barnes, 1946.

"Anti-Semite and Jew," translated from *Réflexions sur la Question Juive* by Paul Morihien. Copyright © 1948 by Schocken Books, Inc.

"Why Does One Write?" translated from *Situations II*: "Qu'est-ce que la littérature?" by Bernard Frechtman, 1948.

"Saint Genet," translated from *Saint Genêt: Comédien et Martyr* by Bernard Frechtman. Copyright © 1963 by George Braziller, Inc.

"The Colonizer and the Colonized," translated from the "Introduction" to Albert Memmi's *Portrait du Colonisé précédé du Portrait du Colonisateur* by Lawrence Hoey. Copyright © 1965 by The Orion Press, Inc.

"Search for a Method," translated from "Question de Méthode," the prefatory essay in *Critique de la Raison Dialectique,* Volume I, by Hazel E. Barnes. Copyright © 1963 by Alfred A. Knopf.

THE MEANING OF EXISTENCE: NAUSEA

The word absurdity is coming to life under my pen; a little while ago, in the garden, I couldn't find it, but neither was I looking for it, I didn't need it: I thought without words, *on* things, *with* things. Absurdity was not an idea in my head, or the sound of a voice, only this long serpent dead at my feet, this wooden serpent. Serpent or claw or root or vulture's talon, what difference does it make? And without formulating anything clearly, I understood that I had found the key to Existence, the key to my Nauseas, to my own life. In fact, all that I could grasp beyond that returns to this fundamental absurdity. Absurdity: another word; I struggle against words; down there I touched the thing. But I wanted to fix the absolute character of this absurdity here. A movement, an event in the tiny colored world of men is only relatively absurd: by relation to the accompanying circumstances. A madman's ravings, for example, are absurd in relation to the situation in which he finds himself, but not in relation to his delirium. But a little while ago I made an experiment with the absolute or the absurd. This root—there was nothing in relation to which it was absurd. Oh, how can I put it in words? Absurd: in relation to the stones, the tufts of yellow grass, the dry mud, the tree, the sky, the green benches. Absurd, irreducible; nothing—not even a profound, secret upheaval of nature—could explain it. Evidently I did not know everything, I had not seen the seeds sprout, or the tree

1

grow. But faced with this great wrinkled paw, neither ignorance nor knowledge was important: the world of explanations and reasons is not the world of existence. A circle is not absurd, it is clearly explained by the rotation of a straight segment around one of its extremities. But neither does a circle exist. This root, on the other hand, existed in such a way that I could not explain it. Knotty, inert, nameless, it fascinated me, filled my eyes, brought me back unceasingly to its own existence. In vain to repeat: "This is a root"—it didn't work any more. I saw clearly that you could not pass from its function as a root, as a breathing pump, *to that,* to this hard and compact skin of a sea lion, to this oily, callous, headstrong look. The function explained nothing: it allowed you to understand generally that it was a root, but not *that one* at all. This root, with its color, shape, its congealed movement, was . . . below all explanation. Each of its qualities escaped it a little, flowed out of it, half solidified, almost became a thing; each one was *in the way* in the root and the whole stump now gave me the impression of unwinding itself a little, denying its existence to lose itself in a frenzied excess. I scraped my heel against this black claw: I wanted to peel off some of the bark. For no reason at all, out of defiance, to make the bare pink appear absurd on the tanned leather: to *play* with the absurdity of the world. But, when I drew my heel back, I saw that the bark was still black. . . .

This moment was extraordinary. I was there, motionless and icy, plunged in a horrible ecstasy. But something fresh had just appeared in the very heart of this ecstasy; I understood the Nausea, I possessed it. To tell the truth, I did not formulate my discoveries to myself. But I think it would be easy for me to put them in words now. The essential thing is contingency. I mean that one cannot define existence as necessity. To exist is simply *to be there;* those who exist let themselves be encountered, but you can never deduce anything from them. I believe there are people who have understood this. Only they tried to overcome this contingency by inventing a necessary, causal being. But no necessary being can explain existence: contingency is not a delusion, a probability which can be dissipated; it is the absolute, consequently, the perfect free gift. All is free, this park, this city and myself. When you realize that, it turns your heart upside down and everything begins to float, as the other evening at the "Railwaymen's Rendezvous": here is Nausea; here there is what those bastards—the ones on the Coteau Vert and others—try to hide from themselves with their idea of their rights. But what a poor lie: no one has any rights; they are entirely free, like other men, they cannot succeed in not feeling superfluous. And in themselves, secretly, they are *superfluous,* that is to say, amorphous, vague, and sad.

How long will this fascination last? I *was* the root of the chestnut tree. Or rather I was entirely conscious of its existence. Still detached from it—since I was conscious of it—yet lost in it, nothing but it. An uneasy conscience which, notwithstanding, let itself fall with all its weight on this piece of dead wood. Time had stopped: a small black pool at my feet; it was impossible for something to come *after* that moment. I would have liked to tear myself from that atrocious joy, but I did not even imagine it would be possible; I was inside; the black stump did *not move,* it stayed there, in my eyes, as a lump of food sticks in the windpipe. I could neither accept nor refuse it. At what a cost did I raise my eyes? Did I raise them? Rather did I not obliterate myself for an instant in order to be reborn in the following instant with my head thrown back and my eyes raised upward? In fact, I was not even conscious of the transformation. But suddenly it became impossible for me to think of the existence of the root. It was wiped out, I could repeat in vain: it exists, it is still there, under the bench, against my right foot, it no longer meant anything. Existence is not something which lets itself be thought of from a distance: it must invade you suddenly, master you, weigh heavily on your heart like a great motionless beast—or else there is nothing more at all.

There was nothing more, my eyes were empty and I was spellbound by my deliverance. Then suddenly it began to move before my eyes in light, uncertain motions: the wind was shaking the top of the tree.

It did not displease me to see a movement, it was a change from these motionless beings who watched me like staring eyes. I told myself, as I followed the swinging of the branches: movements never quite exist, they are passages, intermediaries between two existences, moments of weakness, I expected to see them come out of nothingness, progressively ripen, blossom: I was finally going to surprise beings in the process of being born.

No more than three seconds, and all my hopes were swept away. I could not attribute the passage of time to these branches groping around like blind men. This idea of passage was still an invention of man. The idea was too transparent. All these paltry agitations, drew in on themselves, isolated. They overflowed the leaves and branches everywhere. They whirled about these empty hands, enveloped them with tiny whirlwinds. Of course a movement was something different from a tree. But it was still an absolute. A thing. My eyes only encountered completion. The tips of the branches rustled with existence which unceasingly renewed itself and which was never born. The existing wind rested on the tree like a great bluebottle, and the tree shuddered. But the shudder was not a nascent quality, a passing from power to action; it was a thing; a shudder-thing flowed into the tree, took possession of it, shook it and suddenly abandoned it, going further on to spin about itself. All was fullness and all was active, there was no weakness in time;

all, even the least perceptible stirring, was made of existence. And all these existents which bustled about this tree came from nowhere and were going nowhere. Suddenly they existed no longer: existence is without memory; of the vanished it retains nothing—not even a memory. Existence everywhere, infinitely, in excess, for ever and everywhere; existence—which is limited only by existence. I sank down on the bench, stupefied. . . . It didn't make sense, the World was everywhere, in front, behind. There had been nothing *before* it. Nothing. There had never been a moment in which it could not have existed. That was what worried me: of course there was no *reason* for this flowing larva to exist. *But it was impossible* for it not to exist. It was unthinkable: to imagine nothingness you had to be there already, in the midst of the World, eyes wide open and alive; nothingness was only an idea in my head, an existing idea floating in this immensity: this nothingness had not come *before* existence, it was an existence like any other and appeared after many others. I shouted "filth! what rotten filth!" and shook myself to get rid of this sticky filth, but it held fast and there was so much, tons and tons of existence, endless: I stifled at the depths of this immense weariness. And then suddenly the park emptied as through a great hole, the World disappeared as it had come, or else I woke up—in any case, I saw no more of it; nothing was left but the yellow earth around me, out of which dead branches rose upward.

I got up and went out. Once at the gate, I turned back. Then the garden smiled at me. I leaned against the gate and watched for a long time. The smile of the trees, of the laurel, *meant* something; that was the real secret of existence. I remembered one Sunday, not more than three weeks ago, I had already detected everywhere a sort of conspiratorial air. Was it in my intention? I felt with boredom that I had no way of understanding. No way. Yet it was there, waiting, looking at one. It was there on the trunk of the chestnut tree . . . it was *the* chestnut tree. Things—you might have called them thoughts—which stopped halfway, which were forgotten, which forgot what they wanted to think and which stayed like that, hanging about with an odd little sense which was beyond them. That little sense annoyed me: I *could not* understand it, even if I could have stayed leaning against the gate for a century; I had learned all I could know about existence. I left, I went back to the hotel and I wrote.

FREEDOM TO CREATE: THE PSYCHOLOGY
OF IMAGINATION

1. *Consciousness and Imagination*

What are the characteristics that can be attributed to consciousness from the fact that it is a consciousness capable of *imagining?* This question can be taken in the sense of a critical analysis under the form: what must be the nature of consciousness in general in order that the construction of an image should always be possible? And, no doubt, it is under this form that our minds, accustomed to raising philosophical questions in the Kantian perspective, will best understand it. But, as a matter of fact, the problem in its deepest meaning can only be grasped from a phenomenological point of view.

After the phenomenological reduction we find ourselves in the presence of the transcendental consciousness which unveils itself to our reflective descriptions. We can thus fix by concepts the result of our eidetic intuition of the essence "consciousness." Now, phenomenological descriptions can discover, for instance, that the very structure of the transcendental consciousness implies that this consciousness is constitutive *of a world.* But it is evident that they will not teach us that consciousness must be constitutive *of* such a world, that is exactly the one where we are, with its earth, its animals, its men and the story of these men. We are here in the presence of a primary and irreducible fact which presents itself as a contingent and irrational specification of the noematic essence of the *world*. And many phenomenologists will call "metaphysics" the investigation whose aim it is to uncover this contingent existent in its entirety. This is not exactly what we would call metaphysics, but this is of little importance here. What will concern us here is this: is the imaginary function a contingent and metaphysical specification of the essence "consciousness" or should it rather be described as a constitutive structure of that essence? In other words: can we conceive of a consciousness which would never imagine and which would be completely absorbed in its intuitions of the real—in that case the possibility of imagining, which appear as one quality among others of *our* consciousnesses, would be a contingent enrichment—or rather, as soon as we posit a consciousness, must it be posited as always being able to imagine? This question should be able to settle itself by the simple reflective inspection of the essence "consciousness" and it is thus in fact that we would attempt to settle it, were we not addressing ourselves to a public as yet but little accustomed to phenomenological methods. But since the idea of eidetic intuition is still repugnant to many French readers, we shall resort to a subterfuge, that is, to a method somewhat more complex. We shall begin with the question: what must a consciousness be in order for it to possess the power to imagine, which we shall try to develop by the usual procedures of critical analysis, that is, by a regressive method. Next we shall compare the results we obtain with those the Cartesian intuition gives us of the consciousness realized by the cogito and we shall see whether the necessary conditions for realizing an imaginative consciousness are *the same* or *different* from the conditions of possibility of a consciousness in general.

In truth, the problem stated thus may appear to be completely new and even trifling to French psychologists. And, in fact, as long as we are the victims of the illusion of immanence, there is no general problem of imagination. Images are in fact supplied in these theories by a type of existence strictly like that of things. They are reborn sensations which may differ in degree, in cohesion, in meaning from primary sensations but which belong, as do sensations, to *intra-mundane* existence. The image is as real as any other existence. The only question concerning the image is the problem of its relationship to other existences but whatever this relationship may be, the existence of the image remains intact. This is like saying that whether the portrait of King Charles VI is or is not a true likeness, whether the king is dead or alive or even whether he ever existed, the portrait is nevertheless something that exists in the world. There is therefore no existential problem of the image.

But . . . the existential problem of the image can no longer be sidetracked. In fact, to the existence of an object for consciousness there corresponds noetically a hypothesis or position of existence. Now, the hypothesis of the imaginative consciousness is radically different from the hypothesis of a consciousness of the real. This means that the type of existence of the object of the image *as long as it is imagined,* differs in nature from the type of existence of the object grasped as real. And, surely, if I now form an image of Peter, my imaginative consciousness includes a certain position of the existence of Peter, insofar as he is now at this very moment in Berlin or London. But while he *appears to me as an image,* this Peter who is in London *appears to me absent.* This absence in actuality, this essential nothingness of the imagined object is enough to distinguish it from the object of perception. What then must be the nature of a consciousness in order that it be able to successively posit *real* objects and *imagined* objects?

We must at once make an important observation, which

the reader could have made himself if he had studied with us the problem of the relationships between perception and imagery. For an object or any element of an object there is very much of a difference between *being envisioned as nothing* and *being given-as-absent.* In a perception of whatever sort many empty intentions are directed, from the elements of the object now given, towards other aspects and other elements of the object which no longer reveal themselves to our intuition. For instance, the arabesques of the rug I am viewing are both in part given to my intuition. The legs of the armchair which stands before the window conceal certain curves, certain designs. But I nevertheless seize these hidden arabesques as *existing now,* as hidden but not at all as absent. And I grasp them not for themselves in trying to present them by means of an analogue but in the very way in which I grasp what has been given me of their continuation. I *perceive* the beginnings and the endings of the hidden arabesques (which appear to me in front and in back of the leg of the chair) as *continuing* under the legs of chair. It is therefore *in the way in which I grasp the data* that I posit that which is not given as being real. Real by the same right as the data, as that which gives it its meaning and its very nature. Likewise the successive tones of a melody are grasped by appropriate retentions as that which makes of the tone now heard exactly what it is. In this sense, to perceive this or that real datum is to perceive it on the foundation of total reality *as a whole.* This reality does not make the object of any special act of my attention but it is co-present as an essential condition of the existence of the reality actually perceived. Here we see that the imaginative act is the reverse of the act of reality. If I want to imagine the hidden arabesques, I direct my attention upon them and I isolate them, just as I isolate on a foundation of an undifferentiated universe the thing I now see. I cease to grasp them in a vacuum

10

as constituting the sense of the perceived reality, *I present them to myself,* in themselves, but precisely as I cease to envision them from the beginning of a present, in order to grasp them by themselves, I grasp them as *absent,* they appear to me as empty data. Of course they really exist yonder under the chair and it is yonder that I envision them but precisely as I envision them where they are not given to me I grasp them as a nothing for me. Thus the imaginative act is at once *constituting, isolating* and *annihilating.*

It is this which turns the problem of memory and that of anticipation into two problems which are radically different from the problem of imagination. No doubt but that recollection is in many respects very close to the image and at times we were able to draw our examples from memory to clarify the nature of the image. There is nevertheless an essential difference between the theme of recollection and that of the image. If I recall an incident of my past life I do not imagine it, I *recall* it. That is, I do not posit it as *given-in-its-absence,* but as *given-now-as-in-the-past.* The handshake of Peter of last evening in leaving me did not turn into an unreality as it became a thing of the past; it simply *went into retirement;* it is always real but *past.* It exists *past,* which is one mode of real existence among others. And when I want to apprehend it anew I envision it *where it is,* I direct my consciousness towards that past object which is *yesterday* and at the heart of that object. I recover the event I am looking for, the handshake of Peter. In a word, just as when I want to *see* actually the hidden arabesques under the chair I have to look for them where they are, that is, remove the chair; so when I recall this or that memory I do not *call it forth* but I betake myself where it is, I direct my consciousness to the past where it awaits me as a real event in retirement. But if I imagine Peter as he might be at that moment in Berlin—or simply Peter as he exists at that moment (and not as he was yesterday on leaving me), I grasp an object which is not at all given to me or which is given to me simply as being beyond reach. There I grasp *nothing*, that is, I posit *nothingness*. In this sense the imaginative consciousness of Peter in Berlin (what is he doing at this moment? I imagine he is walking in the Kurfürstendamm, etc.), is very much closer to that of the centaur (whose complete inexistence I proclaim), than the recollection of Peter as he was the day he left. What is common between Peter as an image and the Centaur as an image is that they are two aspects of Nothingness. And this it is that also distinguishes the living future from the imagined future. There are in fact two sorts of Futures: the one is but the temporal ground on which my present perception develops, the other is posited for itself but as *that which is not yet*. When I play tennis I see my opponent hit the ball with his racket and I run to the net. Here there is real anticipation since I foresee the course of the ball. But this anticipation does not posit for itself the passage of the ball to this or that point. In reality the future is here but the *real* development of a form induced by the gesture of my opponent and the real gesture of this opponent communicates its reality to the whole form. In other words, the real form with its zones of real-past and real-future is effected entirely as a result of his gesture. *As for my prevision also being reality,* I continue to carry out the form by foreseeing it, because my prevision is a real gesture within the form. Thus, step by step, there is always a real future which occurs simply as the real past, the sense of an actual form in development, or in other words, as the meaning of the universe. And, in this sense, it is like presenting the unperceived real aspects of objects as a present which is real and envisioned in a vacuum, or as a real future. The arabesques hidden by the chair are also the real complement of the gesture by which I remove the chair as the present and latent existence hidden by the chair. All real existence occurs with present, past and future structures, therefore past and future as essential structures of the real, are also real, that is, correlatives of a realizing theme. But if, on the contrary, while lying on my bed I anticipate what might happen when my friend Peter returns from Berlin, I detach the future from the present whose meaning it constitutes. I posit it for itself and I present it to myself. But I give it to myself exactly while it is not yet, that is as absent, or if one prefers, as nothing. Thus, I can live the same future in reality as a ground of the present (as, for instance, I look for Peter at the station and all my acts have for their real meaning the arrival of Peter at 7:35 P.M.), or on the contrary isolate it and posit it for itself but by cutting it off from all reality and by annihilating it, by *presenting it as nothingness.*

We now can see what the essential requisite is in order that a consciousness may be able to imagine; it must have the possibility of positing an hypothesis of unreality. But we must clarify this requisite. It does not mean that consciousness must cease being consciousness *of* something. It is of the very nature of consciousness to be intentional and a consciousness that would cease to be consciousness of something would for that very reason cease to exist. But consciousness should be able to form and posit objects possessing a certain trait of nothingness in relation to the whole of reality. In fact, we recall that the imaginary object can be posited as non-existent or as absent or as existing elsewhere or not posited as existing. We note that the common property of these four is that they include the entire category of negation, though at different degrees. Thus the negative act is constitutive of the image. We have already mentioned, in fact, that the theme is not added to the image but that it is its most intimate structure. But in relation to what is the negation carried out? To answer this question we need but

13

consider for a moment what happens when I grasp the portrait of Charles VIII as *an* image of Charles VIII. At one stroke I stop to consider the picture as forming a part of a real world. It is no longer possible that the perceived object *on* the picture can be changed by the changes of the milieu surrounding it. The picture itself, as a *real thing,* can be more or less brightened, its colors can peel off, it can burn. This is because it possesses—due to lack of a "being-in-the-world" which is restricted to consciousness—a "being-in-the-midst-of-the-world." Its objective nature depends upon reality grasped as a spatio-temporal whole. But if, on the contrary, I grasp Charles VIII as an image on the picture, the object apprehended can no longer be subjected for instance to changes in brightness. It is not true that I can more or less brighten the *cheek* of Charles VIII.

The brightening of that cheek has been, in fact, once and for all, established in the unreal by the painter. It is the unreal sun—or the unreal candle placed by the painter at this or that distance from the face being painted—which determines the degree of the brightness of the cheek. All that a real projector can do is to brighten the part of the real picture that corresponds to the cheek of Charles VIII. Likewise, if the picture burns—it is not Charles VIII as an image who is burning but only the material object which serves as analogue for the manifestation of the imagined object. Thus the unreal object appears at one stroke to be beyond the reach of reality. We therefore see that in order to produce the object "Charles VIII" as an image consciousness must be able to deny the reality of the picture and that it could deny that reality only by retreating from reality grasped in its totality. To posit an image is to construct an object on the fringe of the whole of reality, which means therefore to hold the real at a distance, to free oneself from it, in a word, to deny it. Or, in other words, to deny that an object belongs to the

14

real is to deny the real in positing the object; the two nega-
tions are complementary, the former being the condition for
the latter. We know, besides, that the totality of the real,
so long as it grasped by consciousness as a synthetic *situation*
for that consciousness, is the world. There is then a two-fold
requisite if consciousness is to imagine: it must be able to
posit the world in its synthetic totality, and it must be able
to posit the imagined object as being out of reach of this
synthetic totality, that is, posit the world as a nothingness in
relation to the image. From this it follows clearly that all
creation of the imaginary would be completely impossible to
a consciousness whose nature it would be precisely to be
"in-the-midst-of-the-world." If we assume a consciousness
placed in the very bosom of the world as one existence
among others, we must conceive it hypothetically as completely subjected to the actions of a variety of realities—
without its being able to avoid the detail of these realities
by an intuition which would embrace their totality. This consciousness could therefore contain only real modifications
aroused by real actions and all imagination would be pro-
hibited to it, exactly in the degree to which it would be
engulfed in the real. This conception of an imagination
mired in the world is not unknown to us since it is precisely that of psychological determinism. We can affirm fear-
lessly that if consciousness is a succession of determined
psychical facts it is entirely impossible for it ever to produce
anything but the real. For a consciousness to be able to
imagine it must be able to escape from the world by its very
nature, it must be able by its own efforts to withdraw from
the world. In a word it must be free. Thus the thesis of unreality has yielded us the possibility of negation as its condition. Now, the latter is possible only by the "negation" of
the world as a whole, and this negation has revealed itself
to us as being the reverse of the very freedom of conscious-

ness. But at this point several comments force themselves to the fore: first of all we must bear in mind that the act of positing the world as a synthetic totality and the act of "taking perspective" from the world are both one and the same. If we may use a comparison, it is precisely by placing oneself at a convenient distance from the picture that the impressionist painter disengages the whole "forest" or the "white water lilies" from the multitude of small strokes he has placed on the canvas. But, reciprocally, the possibility of constructing a whole is given as the primary structure of the act of taking perspective. It is therefore enough to be able to posit reality as a synthetic whole in order to posit oneself as free from it and this going-beyond is freedom itself since it could not happen if consciousness were not free. Thus to posit the world as a world or to "negate" it is one and the same thing. In this sense Heidegger can say that nothingness is the constitutive structure of the existent. To be able to imagine, it is enough that consciousness be able to surpass the real in constituting it as a world, since the negating of the real is always implied by its constitution in the world. But this surpassing cannot be brought about by any means whatever, and the freedom of consciousness must not be confused with the arbitrary. For an image is not purely and simply the *world-negated,* it is always *the world negated from a certain point of view,* namely, the one that permits the positing of the absence or the non-existence of the object presented "as an image." The arbitrary position of the real as a world will not of itself cause the appearance of the centaur as an unreal object. For the centaur to emerge as unreal the world must be grasped as a world-where-the-centaur-is-not, and this can only happen if consciousness is led by different motivations to grasp the world as being exactly the sort in which the centaur has no place. Likewise, if my friend Peter is to be given me as absent I must be led to grasp the world as that

16

sort of a whole in which Peter cannot *actually exist* and *be present to me.* (He can actually be present for others—in Berlin, for instance.) What motivates the appearance of the unreal is not necessarily nor most often the *representative* intuition of the world from some point of view. Consciousness as a fact has many other ways of *surpassing the real in order to make a world of it*: the surpassing can and should happen at first by affectivity or by action. The appearance of a dead friend as unreal, for instance, is built on the foundation of affective expectation of the real as an *empty world* from this point of view.

We shall give the name of "situations" to the different immediate ways of apprehending the real as a world. We can therefore say that the essential prerequisite that enables consciousness to imagine is that it be "situated in the world" or more briefly, that it "be-in-the-world." It is the situation-in-the-world, grasped as a concrete and individual reality of consciousness, which is the motivation for the construction of any unreal object whatever and the nature of that unreal object is circumscribed by this motivation. Thus the *situation* of consciousness does not need to appear as a pure and abstract condition of possibility for all imagination but as the concrete and exact motivation for the appearance of a certain particular imagination.

From this point of view we finally grasp the relation between the unreal and the real. At first, even if an image is not produced at this moment, every apprehension of the real as a world tends of its own accord to end up with production of unreal objects because it is always, in one sense, a free negation of the world and that always *from a particular point of view*. Thus, if consciousness is free, the noematic correlative of its freedom should be the *world* which carries in itself its possibility of negation, at each moment and from each point of view, by means of an image, even while the image must as yet be constructed by a particular intention of consciousness. But, reciprocally, an image, being a negation of the world from a particular point of view, can never appear excepting *on the foundation of the world* and in connection with the foundation. Naturally the appearance of the image demands that the particular perceptions should be diluted in the syncretic wholeness *world* and that this wholeness should withdraw. But it is exactly the withdrawal of the wholeness which turns it into a foundation, the foundation on which the unreal form must detach itself. Thus, although as a result of producing the unreal, consciousness can appear momentarily delivered from "being-in-the-world," it is just this "being-in-the-world" which is the necessary condition for the imagination.

Thus the critical analysis of the conditions that made all imagination possible has led us to the following discoveries: in order to imagine, consciousness must be free from all specific reality and this freedom must be able to define itself by a "being-in-the-world" which is at once the constitution and the negation of the world; the concrete situation of the consciousness in the world must at each moment serve as the singular motivation for the constitution of the unreal. Thus the unreal—which is always a two-fold nothingness: nothingness of itself in relation to the world, nothingness of the world in relation to itself—must always be constituted on the foundation of the world which it denies, it being well understood, moreover, that the world does not present itself only to a representative intuition and that this synthetic foundation simply demands to be lived as a situation. If these are the conditions that make imagination possible, do they correspond to a specification, to an enrichment contingent upon the essence "consciousness" or are they nothing else than the very essence of that consciousness considered from a particular point of view? It seems that the answer lies in the question. Indeed, what is this free consciousness whose nature is to be the consciousness *of* something, but which, for this very reason, constructs itself before the real and which surpasses it at each moment because it can exist only by "being-in-the-world," that is, by living its relation to the real as *situation,* what is it, indeed, if not simply consciousness such as it reveals itself to itself in the cogito?

Is doubt the very primary condition of the real as a world and its negation from this same point of view and does not reflective grasp of the doubt coincide with the apodictic intuition of freedom?

We may therefore conclude that imagination is not an empirical and superadded power of consciousness, it is the whole of consciousness as it realizes its freedom; every concrete and real situation of consciousness in the world is big with imagination in as much as it always presents itself as a withdrawing from the real. It does not follow that all perception of the real must reverse itself in imagination, but as consciousness is always "in a situation" because it is always free, it always and at each moment has the concrete possibility of producing the unreal. These are the various motivations which decide at each moment whether consciousness will only be realized or whether it will imagine. The unreal is produced outside of the world by a consciousness which *stays in the world* and it is because he is transcendentally free that man can imagine.

But, in its turn, the imagination, which has become a psychological and empirical function, is the necessary condition for the freedom of empirical man in the midst of the world. For, if the negating function belonging to consciousness—which Heidegger calls surpassing—is what makes the act of imagination possible, it must be added on the other hand that this function can manifest itself only in an imaginative act. There can be no intuition of nothingness just because nothingness is nothing and because all consciousness intuitive or not is consciousness of something. Nothingness can present itself only as an infra-structure of something. The experience of nothingness is not, strictly speaking, an indirect one, it is an experience which is in principle given "with" and "in." The analyses of Bergson are pertinent in this connection: any attempt to directly conceive death or the nothingness of existence is by nature bound to fail.

The gliding of the world into the bosom of nothingness and the emergence of human reality in this very nothingness can happen only through the position of *something* which is nothingness in relation to the world and in relation to which the world is nothing. By this we evidently define the structure of the imagination. It is the appearance of the imaginary before consciousness which permits the grasping of the process of turning the world into nothingness as its essential condition and as its primary structure. If it were possible to conceive for a moment a consciousness which does not imagine, it would have to be conceived as completely engulfed in the existent and without the possibility of grasping anything but the existent. But it is exactly which cannot be nor could be: all existence as soon as it is posited is surpassed by itself. But it must retreat *towards something.* The imaginary is in every case the "something" concrete toward which the existent is surpassed. When the imaginary is not posited as a fact, the surpassing and the nullifying of the existent are swallowed up in the existent; the surpassing and the freedom *are there* but are not revealed; the person is crushed in the world, run through by the real, he is closest to the thing. However, as soon as he apprehends in one way or another (most of the time without representation) the whole as a *situation,* he retreats from it towards that in relation to which he is *a lack,* an *empty space,* etc. In a word, the concrete motivation of the imaginative consciousness itself presupposes the imaginative structure of consciousness; the realizing consciousness always includes a retreat toward a particular imaginative consciousness which is like the reverse of the situation and in relation to which the situation is defined. For instance, if I desire to see my friend Peter who is not here now, the situation defines itself as a "being in the world" such as Peter is not now given, and Peter is this because the whole of the real is surpassed in order to make a world. But it is not at all the real Peter who, on the contrary, if he were given as present or as envisioned on the basis of the real by empty and presentifying intentions (for instance, if I heard his steps outside the door), would be a part of the situation: this Peter in relation to whom the situation becomes defined is exactly the *absent* Peter.

The imaginary thus represents at each moment the implicit meaning of the real. The imaginative act itself consists in positing the imaginary for itself, that is, in making that meaning explicit—as when Peter as an image rises suddenly before me—but this specific position of the imaginary will be accompanied by a collapsing of the world which is then no more than the negated foundation of the unreal. And if the negation is the unconditioned principle of all imagination, it itself can never be realized excepting in and by an act of imagination. That which is denied must be imagined. In fact, the object of a negation cannot be *real* because that would be affirming what is being denied—but neither can it be a complete nothing, since it is *something* that is being denied. So the object of a negation must be posited as imaginary. And this is true for the logical forms of negation (doubt, restriction, etc.) as it is for its active and affective forms (defense, consciousness of impotence, of deprivation, etc.).

Now we are at the point of understanding the meaning and the value of the imaginary. The imaginary appears "on the foundation of the world," but reciprocally all apprehension of the real as a world implies a hidden surpassing towards the imaginary. All imaginative consciousness uses the world as the negated foundation of the imaginary and reciprocally all consciousness of the world calls and motivates an imaginative consciousness as grasped from the particular *meaning* of the situation. The apprehension of nothingness could not occur by an immediate unveiling, it develops in and by the free succession of acts of consciousness, the nothingness is the material of the surpassing of the world towards the imaginary. It is as such that it is *lived,* without ever being posited for itself. There could be no developing consciousness without an imaginative consciousness, and vice versa. So imagination, far from appearing as an *actual* characteristic of consciousness turns out to be an essential and transcendental condition of consciousness. It is as absurd to conceive of a consciousness which would not imagine as it would be to conceive of a consciousness which could not realize the cogito.

2. *The Work of Art*

It is not our intention to deal here with the problem of the work of art in its entirety. Closely related as this problem is to the question of the Imaginary, its treatment calls for a special work in itself. But it is time we drew some conclusions from the long investigations in which we used as an example a statue or the portrait of Charles VIII or a novel. The following comments will be concerned essentially with the existential type of the work of art. And we can at once formulate the law that the work of art is an unreality.

This appeared to us clearly from the moment we took for our example, in an entirely different connection, the portrait of Charles VIII. We understood at the very onset that this Charles VIII was an object. But this, obviously, is not the same object as is the painting, the canvas, which are the real objects of the painting. As long as we observe the canvas and the frame for themselves the esthetic object "Charles VIII" will not appear. It is not that it is hidden by the picture, but because it cannot present itself to a realizing consciousness. It will appear at the moment when consciousness, undergoing a radical change in which the world is negated, will itself become imaginative. The situation here is like that of the cubes which can be seen at will to be five or six in number. It will not do to say that when they are seen as five it is because at that time the aspect of the drawing in which they are six is *concealed*. The intentional act that apprehends them as five is sufficient unto itself, it is complete and *exclusive* of the act which grasps them as six. And so it is with the apprehension of Charles VIII as an image which is depicted on the picture. This Charles VIII on the canvas is necessarily the correlative of the intentional act of an imaginative consciousness. And since this Charles VIII, who is an unreality so long as he is grasped on the canvas, is precisely the object of our esthetic appreciations (it is he who "moves" us, who is "painted with intelligence, power, and grace," etc.), we are led to recognize that, in a picture, the esthetic object is something *unreal*. This is of great enough importance once we remind ourselves of the way in which we ordinarily confuse the real and the imaginary in a work of art. We often hear it said, in fact, that the artist first has an idea in the form of an image which he then *realizes* on canvas. This mistaken notion arises from the fact that the painter can, in fact, begin with a mental image which is, as such, incommunicable, and from the fact that at the end of his labors he presents the public with an object which anyone can observe. This leads us to believe that there occurred a transition from the imaginary to the real. But this is in no way true. That which is real, we must not fail to note, are the results of the brush strokes, the stickiness of the canvas, its grain, the polish spread over the colors. But all this does not constitute the object of esthetic appreciation. What is "beautiful" is something which cannot be experienced as a perception and which, by its very nature, is out of the world. We have just shown that it cannot be *brightened,* for instance, by projecting a light beam on the canvas: it is the canvas that is brightened and not the painting. The fact of the matter is that the painter did not *realize* his mental image at all: he has simply constructed a material analogue of such a kind that everyone can grasp the image provided he looks at the analogue. But the image thus provided with an external analogue remains an image. There is no realization of the imaginary, nor can we speak of its *objectification.* Each stroke of the brush was not made *for itself* nor even for the constructing of a coherent real whole (in the sense in which it can be said that a certain lever in a machine was conceived in the interest of the whole and not for itself). It was given together with an unreal synthetic whole and the aim of the artist was to construct a whole of *real* colors which enable this unreal to manifest itself. The painting should then be conceived as a material thing *visited* from time to time (every time that the spectator assumes the imaginative attitude) by an unreal which is precisely the *painted object.* What deceives us here is the real and sensuous pleasure which certain real colors on the canvas give us. Some reds of Matisse, for instance, produce a sensuous enjoyment in those who see them. But we must understand that this sensuous enjoyment, if thought of in isolation—for instance, if aroused by a color in nature—has nothing of the esthetic. It is purely and simply a pleasure of sense. But when the red of the painting is grasped, it is grasped, in spite of everything, as a part of an unreal whole and it is in this whole that it is beautiful. For instance it is the red of a rug by a table.

There is, in fact, no such thing as pure color. Even if the artist is concerned solely with the sensory relationships between forms and colors, he chooses for that very reason a rug in order to increase the sensory value of the red: tactile elements, for instance, must be intended through the red, it is a *fleecy* red, because the rug is of a fleecy material. Without this "fleeciness" of the color something would be lost. And surely the rug is painted there *for the red* it justifies and not the red for the rug. If Matisse chose a rug rather than a sheet of dry and glossy paper it is because of the voluptuous mixture of the color, the density and the tactile quality of the wool. Consequently the red can be truly enjoyed only in grasping it as the *red of the rug,* and therefore unreal. And he would have lost his strongest contrast with the green of the wall if the green were not rigid and cold, because it is the green of a wall tapestry. It is therefore in the unreal that the relationship of colors and forms takes on its real meaning. And even when drawn objects have their usual meaning reduced to a minimum, as in the painting of the cubists, the painting is at least not flat. The forms we see are certainly not the forms of a rug, a table, nor anything else we see in the world. They nevertheless do have a density, a material, a depth, they bear a relationship of perspective towards each other. They are *things.* And it is precisely in the measure in which they are things that they are unreal. Cubism has introduced the fashion of claiming that a painting should not *represent* or *imitate* reality but should constitute an object in itself. As an aesthetic doctrine such a program is perfectly defensible and we owe many masterpieces to it. But it needs to be understood. To maintain that the painting, although altogether devoid of meaning, nevertheless is a *real* object, would be a grave mistake. It is certainly not an object of nature. The real object no longer functions as an analogue of a bouquet of flowers or a glade. But when I "contemplate" it, I nevertheless am not in a realistic attitude. The painting is still an *analogue*. Only what manifests itself through it is an unreal collection of *new things,* of objects I have never seen or ever will see, but which are not less unreal because of it, objects which do not exist *in the painting,* nor anywhere in the world, but which manifest themselves by means of the canvas, and which have gotten hold of it by some sort of possession. And it is the configuration of these unreal objects that I designate as *beautiful.* The esthetic enjoyment is real but it is not grasped for itself, as if produced by a real color: it is but a manner of apprehending the unreal object and, far from being directed on the real painting, it serves to constitute the imaginary object through the real canvas. This is the source of the celebrated disinterestedness of esthetic experience. This is why Kant was able to say that it does not matter whether the object of beauty, when experienced as beautiful, is or is not objectively real; why Schopenhauer was able to speak of a sort of suspension of the Will. This does not come from some mysterious way of apprehending the real, which we are able to use occasionally. What happens is that the esthetic object is constituted and apprehended by an imaginative consciousness which posits it as unreal.

What we have just shown regarding painting is readily applied to the art of fiction, poetry and drama, as well. It is self-evident that the novelist, the poet and the dramatist construct an unreal object by means of verbal analogues; it is also self-evident that the actor who plays Hamlet makes use of himself, of his whole body, as an analogue of the imaginary person. Even the famous dispute about the paradox of the comedian is enlightened by the view here presented. It is well known that certain amateurs proclaim that the actor *does not believe* in the character he portrays. Others, leaning on many witnesses, claim that the actor becomes identified in some way with the character he is enacting. To us these two views are not exclusive of each other; if by "belief" is meant actually real it is obvious that the actor does not actually consider himself to be Hamlet. But this does not mean that he does not "mobilize" all his powers to make Hamlet real. He uses all his feelings, all his strength, all his gestures as analogues of the feelings and conduct of Hamlet. But by this very fact he takes the reality away from them. *He lives completely in an unreal way.* And it matters little that he is *actually* weeping in enacting the role. These tears, he himself experiences—and so does the audience—as the tears of Hamlet, that is as the analogue of unreal tears. The transformation that occurs here is like that we discussed in the dream: the actor is completely caught up, inspired, by the unreal. It is not the character who becomes real in the actor, it is the actor who *becomes unreal* in his character.

But are there not some arts whose objects seem to escape unreality by their very nature? A melody, for instance, refers to nothing but itself. Is a cathedral anything more than a mass of *real* stone which dominates the surrounding house tops? But let us look at this matter more closely. I listen to a symphony orchestra, for instance, playing the Beethoven Seventh Symphony. Let us disregard exceptional cases— which are besides on the margin of esthetic contemplation— as when I go mainly "to hear Toscanini" interpret Beethoven in his own way. As a general rule what draws me to the concert is the desire "to hear the Seventh Symphony." Of course I have some objection to hearing an amateur orchestra, and prefer this or that well-known musical organization. But this is due to my desire to hear the symphony "played perfectly," because the symphony will then be *perfectly itself.* The shortcomings of a poor orchestra which plays "too fast" or "too slow," "in the wrong tempo," etc., seem to me to rob, to "betray," the work it is playing. At the most the orchestra effaces itself before the work it performs, and, provided I

27

have reasons to trust the performers and their conductor, I am confronted by the symphony itself. This everyone will grant me. But now, what is the Seventh Symphony itself? Obviously it is a *thing,* that is something which is before me, which endures, which lasts. Naturally there is no need to show that that thing is a synthetic whole, which does not consist of tones but of a thematic configuration. But is that "thing" real or unreal? Let us first bear in mind that I am listening to the Seventh Symphony. For me that "Seventh Symphony" does not exist in time, I do not grasp it as a dated event, as an artistic manifestation which is unrolling itself in the Châtelet auditorium on the 17th of November, 1938. If I hear Furtwaengler tomorrow or eight days later conduct another orchestra performing the same symphony, I am in the presence of the same symphony once more. Only it is being played either better or worse. Let us now see *how* I hear the symphony: some persons shut their eyes. In this case they detach themselves from the *visual* and dated event of this particular interpretation: they give themselves up to the pure sounds. Others watch the orchestra or the back of the conductor. But they do not see what they are looking at. This is what Revault d'Allonnes calls reflection with auxiliary fascination. The auditorium, the conductor and even the orchestra have disappeared. I am therefore confronted by the Seventh Symphony, but on the express condition of understanding *nothing about it,* that I do not think of the event as an actuality and dated, and on condition that I listen to the succession of themes as an absolute succession and not as a real succession which is unfolding itself, for instance, on the occasion when Peter paid a visit to this or that friend. In the degree to which I hear the symphony it is *not here,* between these walls, at the tip of the violin bows. Nor is it "in the past" as if I thought: this is the work that matured in the mind of Beethoven on such a date. It is completely beyond the real. It has its own time, that is, it possesses an inner time, which runs from the first tone of the allegro to the last tone of the finale, but this time is not a succession of a preceding time which it continues and which happened "before" the beginning of the allegro; nor is it followed by a time which will come "after" the finale. The Seventh Symphony is in no way *in time*. It is therefore in no way real. It occurs *by itself*, but as absent, as being out of reach. I cannot act upon it, change a single note of it, or slow down its movement. But it depends on the real for its appearance: that the conductor does not faint away, that a fire in the hall does not put an end to the performance. From this we cannot conclude that *the* Seventh Symphony has come to an end. No, we only think that the *performance* of the symphony has ceased. Does this not show clearly that the performance of the symphony is its *analogue?* It can manifest itself only through analogues which are dated and which unroll in our time. But to experience it on those analogues the imaginative reduction must be functioning, that is, the real sounds must be apprehended as analogues. It therefore occurs as a perpetual elsewhere, a perpetual absence. We must not picture it (as does Spandrell in *Point Counterpoint* by Huxley—as so many platonisms) as existing in another world, in an intelligible heaven. It is not only outside of time and space—as are essences, for instance—it is outside of the real, outside of existence. I do not hear it actually, I listen to it in the imaginary. Here we find the explanation for the considerable difficulty we always experience in passing from the world of the theatre or of music into that of our daily affairs. There is in fact no passing from one world into the other, but only a passing from the imaginative attitude to that of reality. Esthetic contemplation is an induced dream and the passing into the real is an actual waking up. We often speak of the "deception" experienced on returning to reality. But this does not explain that this discomfort also exists, for instance, after having witnessed a realistic and cruel play, in which case reality should be experienced as comforting. This discomfort is simply that of the dreamer on awakening; an entranced consciousness, engulfed in the imaginary, is suddenly freed by the sudden ending of the play, of the symphony, and comes suddenly in contact with existence. Nothing more is needed to arouse the nauseating disgust that characterizes the consciousness of reality.

From these few observations we can already conclude that the real is never beautiful. Beauty is a value applicable only to the imaginary and which means the negation of the world in its essential structure. This is why it is stupid to confuse the moral with the esthetic. The values of the Good presume being-in-the-world, they concern action in the real and are subject from the outset to the basic absurdity of existence. To say that we "assume" an esthetic attitude to life is to constantly confuse the real and the imaginary. It does happen, however, that we do assume the attitude of esthetic contemplation towards real events or objects. But in such cases everyone of us can feel in himself a sort of recoil in relation to the object contemplated which slips into nothingness so that, from this moment on, it is no longer *perceived;* it functions as an *analogue* of itself, that is, that an unreal image of what it is appears to us through its actual presence. This image can be purely and simply the object "itself" neutralized, annihilated, as when I contemplate a beautiful woman or death at a bull fight; it can also be the imperfect and confused appearance of *what it could be* through what it is, as when the painter grasps the harmony of two colors as being greater, more vivid, *through* the real blots he finds on a wall. The object at once appears to be *in back of* itself, becomes *untouchable,* it is beyond our reach; and hence arises a sort of sad disinterest in it. It is in this sense that we may say that great beauty in a woman kills the desire for her. In fact we cannot at the same time place ourselves on the plane of the esthetic when this unreal "herself" which we admire appears and on the realistic plane of physical possession. To desire her we must forget she is beautiful, because desire is a plunge into the heart of existence, into what is most contingent and most absurd. Esthetic contemplation of *real* objects is of the same structure as paramnesia, in which the real object functions as analogue of itself in the past. But in one of the cases there is a negating and in the other a placing a thing in the past. Paramnesia differs from the esthetic attitude as memory differs from imagination.

FREEDOM TO HAVE, TO DO, TO BE:
BEING AND NOTHINGNESS

1: *Freedom: The First Condition of Action*

It is strange that philosophers have been able to argue end-lessly about determinism and free-will, to cite examples in favor of one or the other thesis without ever attempting first to make explicit the structures contained in the very idea of *action*. The concept of an act contains, in fact, numerous subordinate notions which we shall have to organize and arrange in a hierarchy: to act is to modify the *shape* of the world; it is to arrange means in view of an end; it is to pro-duce an organized instrumental complex such that by a series of concatenations and connections the modification effected on one of the links causes modifications throughout the whole series and finally produces an anticipated result. But this is not what is important for us here. We should observe first that an action is on principle *intentional*. The careless smoker who has through negligence caused the explosion of a powder magazine has not *acted*. On the other hand the worker who is charged with dynamiting a quarry and who obeys the given orders has acted when he has produced the expected explosion; he knew what he was doing or, if you prefer, he intentionally realized a conscious project.

This does not mean, of course, that one must foresee all the consequences of his act. The emperor Constantine when he established himself at Byzantium, did not foresee that he would create a center of Greek culture and language, the appearance of which would ultimately provoke a schism in the Christian Church and which would contribute to weakening the Roman Empire. Yet he performed an act just in so far as he realized his project of creating a new residence for emperors in the Orient. Equating the result with the intention is here sufficient for us to be able to speak of action. But if this is the case, we establish that the action necessarily implies as its condition the recognition of a "desideratum;" that is, of an objective lack or again of a *négatité*. *The intention* of providing a rival for Rome can come to Constantine only through the apprehension of an objective lack: Rome lacks a counterweight; to this still profoundly pagan city ought to be opposed a Christian city which at the moment *is missing*. Creating Constantinople is understood as an *act* only if first the conception of a new city has preceded the action itself or at least if this conception serves as an organizing theme for all later steps. But this conception can not be the pure representation of the city as *possible*. It apprehends the city in its essential characteristics, which is to be a *desirable* and not yet realized possible.

This means that from the moment of the first conception of the act, consciousness has been able to withdraw itself from the full world of which it is consciousness and to leave the level of being in order frankly to approach that of nonbeing. Consciousness is so far as it is considered exclusively in its being, is perpetually referred from being to being and can not find in being any motive for revealing non-being. The imperial system with Rome as its capital functions positively and in a certain real way which can be easily discovered. Will someone say that the taxes are collected badly, that Rome is not secure from invasions, that it does not have the geographical location which is suitable for the capital of a

Mediterranean empire which is threatened by barbarians, that its corrupt morals make the spread of the Christian religion difficult? How can anyone fail to see that all these considerations are *negative;* that is, that they aim at what is not, not at what is. To say that sixty per cent of the anticipated taxes have been collected can pass, if need be for a positive appreciation of the situation such as it is. To say that the corrupt morals at Rome hinder the spread of Christianity is not to consider this diffusion for what it is; that is, for a propagation at a rate which the reports of the clergy can enable us to determine. It is to posit the diffusion in itself as insufficient; that is, as suffering from a secret nothingness. But it appears as such only if it is surpassed toward a limiting-situation posited *a priori* as a value (for example, toward a certain rate of religious conversions, toward a certain mass morality). This limiting-situation can not be conceived in terms of the simple consideration of the real state of things; for the most beautiful girl in the world can offer only what she *has,* and in the same way the most miserable situation can by itself be designated only as it *is* without any reference to an ideal nothingness.

In so far as man is immersed in the historical situation, he does not even succeed in conceiving of the failures and lacks in a political organization or determined economy; this is not, as is stupidly said, because he "is accustomed to it," but because he apprehends it in its plenitude of being and because he can not even imagine that he can exist in it otherwise. For it is necessary here to reverse common opinion and on the basis of what it is not, to acknowledge the harshness of a situation or the suffering which it imposes, both of which are motives for conceiving of another state of affairs in which things would be better for everybody. It is on the day that we can conceive of a different state of affairs that a new light falls on our troubles and our suffering and that we *decide* that these are unbearable. A worker in 1830 is capable of revolting if his salary is lowered, for he easily conceives of a situation in which his wretched standard of living would be not as low as the one which is about to be imposed on him. But he does not represent his sufferings to himself as unbearable; he adapts himself to them not through resignation but because he lacks the education and reflection necessary for him to conceive of a social state in which these sufferings would not exist. Consequently *he does not act*. Masters of Lyon following a riot, the workers at Croix-Rousse do not know what to do with their victory; they return home bewildered, and the regular army has no trouble in overcoming them. Their misfortunes do not appear to them "habitual" but rather *natural;* they *are,* that is all, and they constitute the worker's condition. They are not detached; they are not seen in the clear light of day, and consequently they are integrated by the worker with his being. He suffers without considering his suffering and without conferring value upon it. To suffer and to *be* are one and the same for him. His suffering is the pure affective tenor of his non-positional consciousness, but he does not *contemplate* it. Therefore this suffering can not be in itself a *motive* for his acts. Quite the contrary, it is after he has formed the project of changing the situation that it will appear intolerable to him. This means that he will have had to give himself room, to withdraw in relation to it, and will have to have effected a double nihilation: on the other hand, he must posit an ideal state of affairs as a pure *present* nothingness; on the other hand, he must posit the actual situation as nothingness in relation to this state of affairs. He will have to conceive of a happiness attached to his class as a pure possible—that is, presently as a certain nothingness—and on the other hand, he will return to the present situation in order to illuminate it in the light of this nothingness and in order to nihilate it in turn by declaring: "I *am not* happy." . . .

In our attempt to reach to the heart of freedom we may be helped by the few observations which we have made on the subject in the course of this work and which we must summarize here. In the first chapter we established the fact that if negation comes into the world through human-reality, the latter must be a being who can realize a nihilating rupture with the world and with himself; and we established that the permanent possibility of this rupture is the same as freedom. But on the other hand, we stated that this permanent possibility of nihilating what I am in the form of "having-been" implies for a man a particular type of existence. We were able then to determine by means of analyses like that of bad faith that human reality is its own nothingness. For the for-itself, to be is to nihilate the in-itself which it is. Under these conditions freedom can be nothing other than this nihilation. It is through this that the for-itself escapes its being as its essence; it is through this that the for-itself is always something other than what can be *said* of it. For in the final analysis the For-itself is the one which escapes this very denomination, the one which is already beyond the name which is given to it, beyond the property which is recognized in it. To say that the for-itself has to be what it is, to say that it is what it is not while not being what it is, to say that in it existence precedes and conditions essence or inversely according to Hegel, that for it "Wesen ist was gewesen ist"—all this is to say one and the same thing: to be aware that man is free. Indeed by the sole fact that I am conscious of the causes which inspire my action, these causes are already transcendent objects for my consciousness; they are outside. In vain shall I seek to catch hold of them; I escape them by my very existence. I am condemned to exist forever beyond my essence, beyond the causes and motives of my act. I am condemned to be free. This means that no limits to my freedom can be found except freedom itself or, if you prefer, that we are not free to cease being free. To the extent that the for-itself wishes to hide its own nothingness from itself and to incorporate the in-itself as its true mode of being, it is trying also to hide its freedom from itself.

The ultimate meaning of determinism is to establish within us an unbroken continuity of existence in itself. The motive conceived as a psychic fact—*i.e.,* as a full and given reality—is, in the deterministic view, articulated without any break with the decision and the act, both of which are equally conceived as psychic givens. The in-itself has got hold of all these "data"; the motive provokes the act as the physical cause its effect; everything is real, everything is full. Thus the refusal of freedom can be conceived only as an attempt to apprehend oneself as being-in-itself; it amounts to the same thing. Human reality may be defined as a being such that in its being its freedom is at stake because human reality perpetually tries to refuse to recognize its freedom. Psychologically in each one of us this amounts to trying to take the causes and motives as *things.* We try to confer permanence upon them. We attempt to hide from ourselves that their nature and their weight depend each moment on the meaning which I give to them; we take them for constants. This amounts to considering the meaning which I gave to them just now or yesterday—which is irremediable because it is *past*—and extrapolating from it a character fixed still in the present. I attempt to persuade myself that the cause *is* as it was. Thus it would pass whole and untouched from my past consciousness to my present consciousness. It would inhabit my consciousness. This amounts to trying to give an essence to the for-itself. In the same way people will posit ends as transcendences,

37

which is not an error. But instead of seeing that the transcendences there posited are maintained in their being by my own transcendence, people will assume that I encounter them upon my surging up in the world; they come from God, from nature, from "my" nature, from society. These ends ready made and pre-human will therefore define the meaning of my act even before I conceive it, just as causes as pure psychic givens will produce it without my even being aware of them.

Cause, act, and end constitute a *continuum*, a *plenum*. These abortive attempts to stifle freedom under the weight of being (they collapse with the sudden upsurge of anguish before freedom) show sufficiently that freedom in its foundation coincides with the nothingness which is at the heart of man. Human-reality is free because it *is not enough.* It is free because it is perpetually wrenched away from itself and because it has been separated by a nothingness from what it is and from what it will be. It is free, finally, because its present being is itself a nothingness in the form of the "reflection-reflecting." Man is free because he is not himself but presence to himself. The being which is what it is can not be free. Freedom is precisely the nothingness which *is made-to-be* at the heart of man and which forces human-reality *to make itself* instead of *to be.* As we have seen, for human reality, to be is to *choose oneself;* nothing comes to it either from the outside or from within which it can *receive or accept.* Without any help whatsoever, it is entirely abandoned to the intolerable necessity of making itself be—down to the slightest detail. Thus freedom is not a being; it is *the being* of man—*i.e.,* his nothingness of being. If we start by conceiving of man as a plenum, it is absurd to try to find in him afterwards moments or psychic regions in which he would be free. As well look for emptiness in a container which one has filled beforehand up to the brim! Man can not be sometimes slave and sometimes free; he is wholly and forever free or he is not free at all. . . .

But this is not all: the will, far from being the unique or at least the privileged manifestation of freedom, actually —like every event of the for-itself—must presuppose the foundation of an original freedom in order to be able to constitute itself as will. The will in fact is posited as a reflective decision in relation to certain ends. But it does not create these ends. It is rather a mode of being in relation to them: it decrees that the pursuit of these ends will be reflective and deliberative. Passion can posit the same ends. For example, if I am threatened, I can run away at top speed because of my fear of dying. This passional fact nevertheless posits implicitly as a supreme end the value of life. Another person in the same situation will, on the contrary, understand that he must remain at his post even if resistance at first appears more dangerous than flight; he "will stand firm." But his goal, although better understood and explicitly posited, remains the same as in the case of the emotional reaction. It is simply that the methods of attaining it are more clearly conceived; certain of them are rejected as dubious or inefficacious, others are more solidly organized. The difference here depends on the choice of means and on the degree of reflection and of making explicit, not on the end. Yet the one who flees is said to be "passionate," and we reserve the term "voluntary" for the man who resists. Therefore the question is of a difference of subjective attitude in relation to a transcendent end. But if we wish to avoid the error which we denounced earlier and not consider these transcendent ends as prehuman and as an *a priori* limit to our transcendence, then we are indeed compelled to recognize that they are the temporalizing projection of our freedom. Human reality can not receive its ends, as we have seen, either from outside or from a so-called inner "nature." It chooses them and by this very choice confers upon them a transcendent existence as the external limit of its projects. From this point of view —and if it is understood that the existence of the *Dasein* precedes and commands its essence—human reality in and through its very upsurge decides to define its own being by its ends. It is therefore the positing of my ultimate ends which characterizes my being and which is identical with the sudden thrust of the freedom which is mine. And this thrust is an *existence;* it has nothing to do with an essence or with a property of a being which would be engendered conjointly with an idea.

Thus since freedom is identical with my existence, it is the foundation of ends which I shall attempt to attain either by the will or by passionate efforts. Therefore it can not be limited to voluntary acts. Volitions, on the contrary, like passions are certain subjective attitudes by which we attempt to attain the ends posited by original freedom. By original freedom, of course, we should not understand a freedom which would be *prior* to the voluntary or passionate act but rather a foundation which is strictly contemporary with the will or the passion and which these *manifest,* each in its own way. Neither should we oppose freedom to the will or to passion as the "profound self" of Bergson is opposed to the superficial self; the for-itself is wholly selfness and can not have a "profound self," unless by this we mean certain transcendent structures of the psyche. Freedom is nothing but the *existence* of our will or of our passions in so far as this existence is the nihilation of facticity; that is, the existence of a being which is its being in the mode of having to be it. We shall return to this point. In any case let us remember that the will is determined within the compass of motives and ends already posited by the for-itself in a transcendent projection of itself toward its possibles. If this were not so, how could we understand deliberation, which is an evaluation of means in relation to already existing ends?

If these ends are already posited, then what remains to be decided at each moment is the way in which I shall conduct myself with respect to them; in other words, the attitude which I shall assume. Shall I act by volition or by passion? Who can decide except me? In fact, if we admit that circumstances decide for me (for example, I can act by volition when faced with a minor danger but if the peril increases, I shall fall into passion), we thereby suppress all freedom. It would indeed be absurd to declare that the will is autonomous when it appears but that external circumstances strictly determine the moment of its appearance. But, on the other hand, how can it be maintained that a will which does not yet exist can suddenly decide to shatter the chain of the passions and suddenly stand forth on the fragments of these chains? Such a conception would lead us to consider the will as a *power* which sometimes would manifest itself to consciousness and at other times would remain hidden, but which would in any case possess the permanence and the existence "in-itself" of a property. This is precisely what is inadmissible. It is, however, certain that common opinion conceives of the moral life as a struggle between a will-thing and passion-substances. There is here a sort of psychological Manichaeism which is absolutely insupportable.

Actually it is not enough to will; it is necessary to will to will. Take, for example, a given situation: I can react to it emotionally. Emotion is not a physiological tempest but a reply adapted to the situation; it is a type of conduct, the meaning and form of which are the object of an intention of consciousness which aims at attaining a particular end

41

by particular means. In fear, fainting and cataplexy aim at suppressing the danger by suppressing the consciousness of the danger. There is an *intention* of losing consciousness in order to do away with the formidable world in which consciousness is engaged and which comes into being through consciousness. Therefore we have to do with magical behavior provoking the symbolic satisfactions of our desires and revealing by the same stroke a magical stratum of the world. In contrast to this conduct voluntary and rational conduct will consider the situation scientifically, will reject the magical, and will apply itself to realizing determined series and instrumental complexes which will enable us to resolve the problems. It will organize a system of means by taking its stand on instrumental determinism. Suddenly it will reveal a technical world; that is, a world in which each instrumental-complex refers to another larger complex and so on. But what will make me decide to choose the magical aspect or the technical aspect of the world? It can not be the world itself, for this in order to be manifested waits to be discovered. Therefore it is necessary that the for-itself in its project must choose being the one by whom the world is revealed as magical or rational; that is, the for-itself must as a free project of itself give to itself magical or rational existence. It is responsible for either one, for the for-itself can *be* only if it has chosen itself. Therefore the for-itself appears as the free foundation of its emotions as of its volitions. My fear *is* free and manifests my freedom; I have put all my freedom into my fear, and I have chosen myself as fearful in this or that circumstance. Under other circumstances I shall exist as deliberate and courageous, and I shall have put all my freedom into my courage. In relation to freedom there is no privileged psychic phenomenon. All my "modes of being" manifest freedom equally since they are all ways of being my own nothingness. . . .

This brief study does not attempt to exhaust the question of the will; on the contrary, it would be desirable to attempt a phenomenological description of the will for itself. But this is not our goal; we hope simply that we have shown that the will is not a privileged manifestation of freedom but that it is a psychic event of a peculiar structure which is constituted on the same plane as other psychic events and which is supported, neither more nor less than the others, by an original ontological freedom.

By the same token freedom appears as an unanalyzable totality; causes, motives, and ends, as well as the mode of apprehending causes, motives, and ends, are organized in a unity within the compass of this freedom and must be understood in terms of it. Does this mean that one must view freedom as a series of capricious jerks comparable to the Epicurean clinamen? Am I free to wish anything whatsoever at any moment whatsoever? And must I at each instant when I wish to explain this or that project encounter the irrationality of a free and contingent choice? Inasmuch as it has seemed that the recognition of freedom had as its consequence these dangerous conceptions which are completely contradictory to experience, worthy thinkers have turned away from a belief in freedom. One could even state that determinism—if one were careful not to confuse it with fatalism—is "more human" than the theory of free will. In fact while determinism throws into relief the strict conditioning of our acts, it does at least give the reason for each of them. And if it is strictly limited to the psychic, if it gives up looking for a conditioning in the ensemble of the universe, it shows that the reason for our acts is in ourselves: we act as we are, and our acts contribute to making us. . . .

We grant to the psychoanalysts that every human reaction is *a priori* comprehensible. But we reproach them for having misunderstood just this initial "comprehensibility" as is shown by their trying to explain the reaction under consideration by means of a prior reaction, which would reintroduce causal mechanism; comprehension must be otherwise defined. Every project is comprehensible as a project of itself toward a possible. It is comprehensible first in so far as it offers a rational content which is immediately apprehensible —I place my knapsack on the ground *in order to* rest for a moment. This means that we immediately apprehend the possible which it projects and the end at which it aims. In the second place it is comprehensible in that the possible under consideration refers to other possibles, these to still others, and so on to the ultimate possibility which I am. The comprehension is effected in two opposed senses: by a regressive psychoanalysis one ascends back from the considered act to my ultimate possible; and by a synthetic progression one redescends from this ultimate possible to the considered act and grasps its integration in the total form.

This form which we call our ultimate possibility is not just *one* possible among others—not even though it be, as Heidegger claims, the possibility of dying or of "no longer realizing any presence in the world." Every particular possibility, in fact, is articulated in an ensemble. It is necessary to conceive of this ultimate possibility as the unitary synthesis of all our actual possibles; each of these possibles resides in an undifferentiated state in the ultimate possibility until a particular circumstance comes to throw it into relief without, however, thereby suppressing its quality of belonging to the totality. Indeed, the perceptive apprehension of any object whatsoever is effected on the *ground of the world*. By this we meant that what the psychologists are accustomed to call "perception" can not be limited to objects which are strictly "seen" or "understood" *etc.* at a certain instant but that the objects considered refer by means of implications and various significations to the totality of the existent in-itself *from the standpoint of which* they are apprehended. Thus it is not true that I proceed by degrees from that table to the room where I am and then going out pass from there to the hall, to the stairway, to the street in order finally to conceive as the result of a passage to the limit, the world as the sum of all existents. Quite the contrary, I can not perceive any instrumental thing whatsoever unless it is in terms of the absolute existence of all existents, for my first being is being-in-the-world.

Thus we find that for man in so far as *"there are" things,* there is in things a perpetual appeal toward the integration which makes us apprehend things by descending from the total integration which is immediately realized down to this particular structure which is interpreted only in relation to this totality. But on the other hand if *there is a world,* it is because we rise up into the world suddenly and in totality. We have observed, in fact, in that same chapter devoted to transcendence, that the in-itself by itself alone is not capable of any unity as a world. But our upsurge is a passion in the sense that we lose ourselves in nihilation in order that a world may exist. Thus the first phenomenon of being in the world is the original relation between the totality of the in-itself or world and my own totality detotalized; I choose myself as a whole in the world which is a whole. Just as I come *from* the world *to* a particular "this," so I come from myself as a detotalized totality to the outline of one of my particular possibilities since I can apprehend a particular "this" on the ground of the world only on the occasion of a particular project of myself. But in this case just as I can apprehend a particular "this" only on the ground of the world by surpassing it toward this or that possibility, so I can project myself beyond the "this" toward this or that possibility only on the ground of my ultimate and total possibility. Thus my ultimate and total possibility, as the original integration of all my particular possibles, and the world as the totality which comes to existents by my upsurge into being are two strictly correlative notions. I can perceive the hammer (*i.e.,* outline a plan of "hammering" with it) only on the ground of the world; but conversely I can outline this act of "hammering" only on the ground of the totality of myself and in terms of that totality.

Thus the fundamental act of freedom is discovered; and it is this which gives meaning to the particular action which I can be brought to consider. This constantly renewed act is not distinct from my being; it is a choice of myself in the world and by the same token it is a discovery of the world. This enables us to avoid the perilous reef of the unconscious which psychoanalysis meets at the start. If nothing is in consciousness which is not a consciousness of being, some will say to us by way of objection that then this fundamental choice must of necessity be a *conscious* choice. They will ask, "Can you maintain that when you yield to fatigue, you are conscious of all the implications which this fact supposes?" We shall reply that we are perfectly conscious of them. Only this consciousness itself must have for its limit the structure of consciousness in general and of the choice which we are making.

So far as the latter is concerned, we must insist on the fact that the question here is not of a deliberate choice. This is not because the choice is *less* conscious or *less* explicit than a deliberation but rather because it is the foundation of all deliberation and because as we have seen, a deliberation requires an interpretation in terms of an original choice. Therefore it is necessary to defend oneself against the illusion which would make of original freedom a *positing* of causes and motives as objects, then a decision from the standpoint of these causes and these motives. Quite the contrary, as soon as there are cause and motive (that is, an appreciation of things and of the structures of the world) there is already a positing of ends and consequently a choice. But this does not mean that the profound choice is thereby unconscious. It is simply one with the consciousness which we have of ourselves. This consciousness, as we know, can be only non-positional; it is we-as-consciousness since it is not distinct from our being. And as our being is precisely our original choice, the consciousness (of) the choice is identical with the self-consciousness which we have. One must be conscious in order to choose, and one must choose in order to be conscious. Choice and consciousness are one and the same thing. This is what many psychologists have felt when they declared that consciousness was "selection." But because they have not traced this selection back to its ontological foundation, they have remained on a level in which the selection appeared as a gratuitous function of a consciousness in other respects substantial. This reproach may in particular be leveled against Bergson. But if it has been well established that consciousness is a nihilation, the conclusion is that to be conscious of ourselves and to choose ourselves are one and the same. This is the explanation of the difficulties which moralizers like Gide have met when they wanted to define the purity of the feelings. What difference is there, Gide asked, between a willed feeling and an *experienced* feeling? Actually there is no difference. "To will to love" and to love are one since to love is to choose oneself as loving by assuming consciousness of loving. If the πάςθo is free, it is a choice. . . .

At the end of this long discussion, it seems that we have succeeded in making a little more precise our ontological understanding of freedom. It will be well at present to gather together and summarize the various results obtained.

(1) A first glance at human reality informs us that for it being is reduced to doing. The psychologists of the nineteenth century who pointed out the "motor" structures of drives, of the attention, of perception, *etc.* were right. But motion itself is an act. Thus we find no *given* in human reality in the sense that temperament, character, passions, principles of reason would be acquired or innate *data* existing in the manner of things. The empirical consideration of the human being shows him as an organized unity of conduct patterns or of "behaviors." To be ambitious, cowardly, or irritable is simply to conduct oneself in this or that matter in this or that circumstance. The Behaviorists were right in considering that the sole positive psychological study ought to be of conduct in strictly defined situations. Just as the work of Janet and the Gestalt School have put us in a position to discover types of emotional conduct, so we ought to speak of types of perceptive conduct since perception is never conceived outside an attitude with respect to the world. Even the disinterested attitude of the scientist, as Heidegger has shown, is the assumption of a disinterested position with regard to the object and consequently one conduct among others. Thus human reality does not exist first in order to act later; but for human reality, to be is to act, and to cease to act is to cease to be.

(2) But if human reality is action, this means evidently that its determination to action is itself action. If we reject this principle, and if we admit that human reality can be determined to action by a prior state of the world or of itself, this amounts to putting a *given* at the beginning of the series. Then these *acts* disappear as acts in order to give place to a series of *movements*. Thus the notion of conduct is itself destroyed with Janet and with the Behaviorists. The existence of the act implies its autonomy.

(3) Furthermore, if the act is not pure motion, it must

be defined by an *intention*. No matter how this intention is considered, it can be only a surpassing of the given toward a result to be obtained. This given, in fact, since it is pure presence, can not get out of itself. Precisely because it is, it is fully and solely what it is. Therefore it can not provide the reason for a phenomenon which derives all its meaning from a result to be attained; that is, from a non-existent. When the psychologists, for example, view the drive as a factual state, they do not see that they are removing from it all its character as an *appetite* (*ad-petitio*). In fact, if the sexual drive can be differentiated from the desire to sleep, for example, this can be only by means of its end, and this end does not exist. Psychologists ought to have asked what could be the ontological structure of a phenomenon such that it makes known to itself what it is by means of something which does not yet exist. The intention, which is the fundamental structure of human-reality, can in no case be explained by a given, not even if it is presented as an emanation from a given. But if one wishes to interpret the intention by its end, care must be taken not to confer on this end an existence as a given. In fact if we could admit that the end is given prior to the result to be attained, it would then be necessary to concede to this end a sort of being-in-itself at the heart of its nothingness and an attractive virtue of a truly magical type. Moreover we should not succeed any better in understanding the connection between a given human reality and a given end than in understanding the connection between consciousness-substance and reality-substance in the realists' arguments. If the drive or the act is to be interpreted by its end, this is because the intention has for its structure *positing* its end outside itself. Thus the intention makes itself be by choosing the end which makes it known.

(4) Since the intention is a choice of the end and since

the world reveals itself across our conduct, it is the intentional choice of the end which reveals the world, and the world is revealed as this or that (in this or that order) according to the end chosen. The end, illuminating the world, is a state *of* the world to be obtained and not yet existing. The intention is a thetic consciousness *of* the end. But it can be so only by making itself a non-thetic consciousness of its own possibility. Thus my *end* can be a good meal if I am hungry. But this meal which beyond the dusty road on which I am traveling is projected as the *meaning* of this road (it *goes toward* a hotel where the table is set, where the dishes are prepared, where I am expected, *etc.*) can be apprehended only correlatively with my non-thetic project toward my own possibility of eating this meal. Thus by a double but unitary upsurge the intention illuminates the world in terms of an end not yet existing and is itself defined by the choice of its possible. My end is a certain objective state of the world, my possible is a certain structure of my subjectivity; the one is revealed to the thetic consciousness, the other flows back over the non-thetic consciousness in order to characterize it.

(5) If the given can not explain the intention, it is necessary that the intention by its very upsurge realize a rupture with the given, whatever this may be. Such must be the case, for otherwise we should have a present plenitude succeeding in continuity a present plenitude, and we could not prefigure the future. Moreover, this rupture is necessary for the *appreciation* of the given. The given, in fact, could never be a *cause* for an action if it were not appreciated. But this appreciation can be realized only by a withdrawal in relation to the given, a putting of the given into parentheses, which exactly supposes a break in continuity. In addition, the appreciation if it is not to be gratuitous, must be effected in the light of something. And this something

which serves to appreciate the given can be only the end. Thus the intention by a single unitary upsurge posits the end, chooses itself, and appreciates the given in terms of the end. Under these conditions the given is appreciated in terms of something which does not yet exist; it is in the light of non-being that being-in-itself is illuminated. There results a double nihilating coloration of the given; on the one hand, it is nihilated in that the rupture makes it lose all efficacy over the intention; on the other hand, it undergoes a new nihilation due to the fact that efficacy is returned to it in terms of a nothingness appreciation. Since human reality is act, it can be conceived only as being at its core a rupture with the given. It is the being which causes *there to be* a given by breaking with it and illuminating it in the light of the not-yet-existing.

(6) The necessity on the part of the given to appear only within the compass of a nihilation which reveals it is actually the same as *internal negation*. . . . It would be in vain to imagine that consciousness can exist without a given; in that case it would be consciousness (of) itself as consciousness of nothing—that is, absolute nothingness. But if consciousness exists in terms of the given, this does not mean that the given conditions consciousness; consciousness is a pure and simple negation of the given, and it exists as the disengagement from a certain existing given and as an engagement toward a certain not yet existing end. But in addition this internal negation can be only the fact of a being which is in perpetual withdrawal in relation to itself. If this being were not its own negation, it would be what it is—*i.e.,* a pure and simple given. Due to this fact it would have no connection with any other *datum* since the given is by nature only what it is. Thus any possibility of the appearance of a world would be excluded. In order not *to be* a given, the for-itself must perpetually constitute itself as in

withdrawal in relation to itself; that is, it must leave itself behind it as a *datum* which it already no longer is. This characteristic of the for-itself implies that it is the being which finds *no help, no pillar of support* in what it *was.* But on the other hand, the for-itself is free and can cause there to be a world because the for-itself is *the being which has to be what it was in the light of what it will be.* Therefore the freedom of the for-itself appears as its *being.* But since this freedom is neither a given nor a property, it can be only by choosing itself. The freedom of the for-itself is always *engaged;* there is no question here of a freedom which could be undetermined and which would pre-exist its choice. We shall never apprehend ourselves except as a choice in the making. But freedom is simply the fact that this choice is always unconditioned.

(7) Such a choice made without base of support and dictating its own causes to itself, can very well appear *absurd,* and in fact it is absurd. This is because freedom is a *choice* of its being but not the *foundation* of its being. We shall return to this relation between freedom and facticity in the course of this chapter. For the moment it will suffice us to say that human-reality can choose itself as it intends but is not able to choose itself. It can not even refuse to be; suicide, in fact, is a choice and affirmation—of being. By this being which is *given* to it, human reality participates in the universal contingency of being and thereby in what we may call absurdity. This choice is absurd, not because it is without reason but because there has never been any possibility of not choosing oneself. Whatever the choice may be, it is founded and reapprehended by being, for it is choice which *is.* But what must be noted here is that this choice is not absurd in the sense in which in a rational universe a phenomenon might arise which would not be bound to others by any *reasons.* It is absurd in this sense—

that the choice is that by which all foundations and all reasons come into being, that by which the very notion of the absurd receives a meaning. It is absurd as being beyond all reasons. Thus freedom is not pure and simple contingency in so far as it turns back toward its being in order to illuminate its being in the light of its end. It is the perpetual escape from contingency; it is the interiorization, the nihilation, and the subjectivizing of contingency, which thus modified passes wholly into the gratuity of the choice.

(8) The free project is fundamental, for it is my being. Neither ambition nor the passion to be loved nor the inferiority complex can be considered as fundamental projects. On the contrary, they of necessity must be understood in terms of a primary project which is recognized as the project which can no longer be interpreted in terms of any other and which is total. A special phenomenological method will be necessary in order to make this initial project explicit. This is what we shall call existential psychoanalysis. We shall speak of this in the next chapter. For the present we can say that the fundamental project which I am is a project concerning not my relations with this or that particular object in the world, but my total being-in-the-world; since the world itself is revealed only in the light of an end, this project posits for its end a certain type of relation to being which the for-itself wills to adopt. This project is not instantaneous, for it can not be "in" time. Neither is it nontemporal in order to "give time to itself" afterwards. That is why we reject Kant's "choice of intelligible character." The structure of the choice necessarily implies that it be a choice in the world. A choice which would be a choice *in terms of nothing,* a choice *against nothing* would be a choice of nothing and would be annihilated as choice. There is only phenomenal choice, provided that we understand that the phenomenon is here the absolute. But in its very up-

surge, the choice is temporalized since it causes a future to come to illuminate the present and to constitute it as a present by giving the meaning of *pastness* to the in-itself "data." However we need not understand by this that the fundamental project is coextensive with the entire "life" of the for-itself. Since freedom is a being-without-support and without-a-springboard, the project in order to be must be constantly renewed. I choose myself perpetually and can never be merely by virtue of having-been-chosen; otherwise I should fall into the pure and simple existence of the in-itself. The necessity of perpetually choosing myself is one with the pursued-pursuit which I am. But precisely because here we are dealing with a *choice,* this choice as it is made indicates in general other choices as possibles. The possibility of these other choices is neither made explicit nor posited, but it is lived in the feeling of unjustifiability; and it is this which is expressed by the fact of the *absurdity* of my choice and consequently of my being. Thus my freedom eats away my freedom. Since I am free, I project my total possible, but I thereby posit that I am free and that I can always nihilate this first project and make it past.

Thus at the moment at which the for-itself thinks to apprehend itself and make known to itself by a projected nothingness what it *is,* it escapes itself; for it thereby posits that it can be other than it is. It will be enough for it to make explicit its unjustifiability in order to cause the *instant* to arise, that is, the appearance of a new project on the collapse of the former. Nevertheless this upsurge of the new project has for its express condition the nihilation of the former, and hence the for-itself can not confer on itself a new existence. As soon as it rejects the project which has lapsed into the past, it has to be this project in the form of the "was"; this means that this lapsed project belongs henceforth to the for-itself's situation. No law of being can assign an *a priori* number to the different projects which I am. The existence of the for-itself in fact conditions its essence. But it is necessary to consult each man's history in order to get from it a particular idea with regard to each individual for-itself. Our particular projects, aimed at the realization in the world of a particular end, are united in the global project which we are. But precisely because we are wholly choice and act, these partial projects are not determined by the global project. They must themselves be choices; and a certain margin of contingency, of unpredictability, and of the absurd is allowed to each of them although each project as it is projected is the specification of the global project on the occasion of particular elements in the situation and so is always understood in relation to the totality of my being-in-the-world.

With these few observations we think that we have described the freedom of the for-itself in its original existence. But it will have been observed that this freedom requires a given, not as its condition but for other sound reasons. First, freedom is conceived only as the nihilation of a given (5); and to the extent that it is an internal negation and a consciousness, it participates (6) in the necessity which prescribes that consciousness be consciousness *of* something. In addition freedom is the freedom of choosing but not the freedom of not choosing. Not to choose is, in fact, to choose not to choose. The result is that the choice is the foundation of being-chosen but not the foundation of choosing. Hence the absurdity (7) of freedom. There again we are referred to a given which is none other than the very facticity of the for-itself. Finally the global project while illuminating the world in its totality can be made specific on the occasion of this or that element of the situation and consequently of the contingency of the world. All these remarks therefore refer us to a difficult problem: that of the relation of freedom to facticity. Moreover we shall inevitably meet other concrete objections. Can I choose to be tall if I am short? To have two arms if I have only one? *etc.* These depend on the "limitations" which my factual situation would impose on my free choice of myself. It will be well therefore to examine the other aspect of freedom, its "reverse side:" its relation to facticity.

2. *Freedom and Facticity: The Situation*

The decisive argument which is employed by common sense against freedom consists in reminding us of our impotence. Far from being able to modify our situation at our whim, we seem to be unable to change ourselves. I am not "free" either to escape the lot of my class, of my nation, of my family, or even to build up my own power or my fortune or to conquer my most insignificant appetites or habits. I am born a worker, a Frenchman, an hereditary syphilitic, or a tubercular. The history of a life, whatever it may be, is the history of a failure. The coefficient of adversity of things is such that years of patience are necessary to obtain the feeblest result. Again it is necessary "to obey nature in order to command it"; that is, to insert my action into the network of determinism. Much more than he appears "to make himself," man seems "to be made" by climate and the earth, race and class, language, the history of the collectivity of which he is a part, heredity, the individual circumstances of his childhood, acquired habits, the great and small events of his life.

This argument has never greatly troubled the partisans of human freedom. Descartes, first of all, recognized both that the will is infinite and that it is necessary "to try to conquer ourselves rather than fortune." Here certain distinctions ought to be made. Many of the facts set forth by the determinists do not actually deserve to enter into our considerations. In particular the coefficient of adversity in things can not be an argument against our freedom, for it is *by us*— *i.e.,* by the preliminary positing of an end—that this coefficient of adversity arises. A particular crag, which manifests a profound resistance if I wish to displace it, will be on the contrary a valuable aid if I want to climb upon it in order to look over the countryside. In itself—if one can even imagine what the crag can be in itself—it is neutral; that is, it waits to be illuminated by an end in order to manifest itself as adverse or helpful. Again it can manifest itself in one or the other way only within an instrumental-complex which is already established. Without picks and piolets, paths already worn, and a technique of climbing, the crag would be neither easy nor difficult to climb; the question would not be posited, it would not support any relation of any kind with the technique of mountain climbing. Thus although brute things (what Heidegger calls "brute existents") can from the start limit our freedom of action, it is our freedom itself which must first constitute the framework, the technique, and the ends in relation to which they will manifest themselves as limits. Even if the crag is revealed as "too difficult to climb," and if we must give up the ascent, let us note that the crag is revealed as such only because it was originally grasped as "climbable"; it is therefore our freedom which constitutes the limits which it will subsequently encounter.

Of course, even after all these observations, there remains an unnamable and unthinkable *residuum which belongs to the in-itself considered* and which is responsible for the fact that in a world illuminated by our freedom, this particular crag will be more favorable for scaling and that one not. But this *residue* is far from being originally a limit for freedom; in fact, it is thanks to this residue—that is, to the brute in-itself as such—that freedom arises as freedom. Indeed common sense will agree with us that the being who is said to be *free* is the one who can *realize* his projects. But in order for the act to be able to allow a *realization,* the simple projection of a possible end must be distinguished *a priori* from the realizations of this end. If conceiving is enough for realizing, then I am plunged in a world like that of a dream in which the possible is no longer in any way distinguished from the real. I am condemned henceforth to see the world modified at the whim of the changes *of* my consciousness; I can not practice in relation to my conception the "putting into brackets" and the suspension of judgment which will distinguish a simple fiction from a real choice. If the object appears as soon as it is simply conceived, it will no longer be chosen or merely wished for. Once the distinction between the simple *wish,* the *representation* which I could choose, and the *choice* is abolished, freedom disappears too. We are free when the final term by which we make known to ourselves what we are is an end; that is, not a real existent like that which in the supposition ¡which we have made could fulfill our wish, but an object which does not yet exist. But consequently this *end* can be transcendent only if it is separated from us at the same time that it is accessible. Only an ensemble of real existents can separate us from this end—in the same way that this end can be conceived only as a state-to-come of the real existents which separate me from it. It is nothing but the outline of an order of existents—that is, a series of dispositions to be assumed by existents on the foundation of their actual relations. By the internal negation, in fact, the for-itself illuminates the existents in their mutual relations by means of the end which it posits, and it projects this end in terms of the determinations which it apprehends in the existent. There is no circle, as we have seen, for the upsurge of the for-itself is effected at one stroke. But if this is the case, then the very order of the existents is indispensable to freedom itself. It is by means of them that freedom is separated from and reunited to the end which it pursues and which makes known to it what it is. Consequently the resistance which freedom reveals in the existent, far from being a danger to freedom, results only in enabling it to arise as freedom. There can be a free for-itself only as engaged in a resisting world. Outside of this engagement the notions of freedom, of determinism, of necessity lose all meaning.

In addition it is necessary to point out to "common sense" that the formula "to be free" does not mean "to obtain what one has wished" but rather "by oneself to determine oneself to wish" (in the broad sense of choosing). In other words success is not important to freedom. The discussion which opposes common sense to philosophers stems here from a misunderstanding: the empirical and popular concept of "freedom" which has been produced by historical, political, and moral circumstances is equivalent to "the ability to obtain the ends chosen." The technical and philosophical concept of freedom, the only one which we are considering here, means only the autonomy of choice. It is necessary, however, to note that the choice, being identical with acting, supposes a commencement of realization in order that the choice may be distinguished from the dream and the wish. Thus we shall not say that a prisoner is always free to go out of prison, which would be absurd, nor that he is always free to long for release, which would be an irrelevant truism, but that he is always free to try to escape (or get himself liberated); that is, that whatever his condition may be, he can project his escape and learn the value of his project by undertaking some action. Our description of freedom, since it does not distinguish between choosing and doing, compels us to abandon at once the distinction between the intention and the act. The intention can no more be separated from the act than thought can be separated from the language which expresses it; and as it happens that our speech informs us of our thought, so our acts will inform us of our intentions—that is, it will enable us to disengage our intentions, to schematize them, and to make objects of them instead of limiting us to living them—*i.e.,* to assume a non-thetic consciousness of them. This essential distinction between the freedom of choice and the freedom of obtaining was certainly perceived by Descartes, following Stoicism. It puts an end to all arguments based on the distinction between "willing" and "being able," which are still put forth today by the partisans and the opponents of freedom.

It is nonetheless true that freedom encounters or seems to encounter limitations on account of the *given* which it surpasses or nihilates. To show that the coefficient of adversity of the thing and its character as an obstacle (joined to its character as an instrument) is indispensable to the existence of a freedom is to use an argument that cuts two ways; for while it enables us to establish that freedom is not invalidated by the given, it indicates, on the other hand, something like an ontological conditioning of freedom. Would it not be reasonable to say, along with certain contemporary philosophers: if no obstacle, then no freedom? And as we can not admit that freedom by itself creates its own obstacle—which would be absurd for anyone who has understood the meaning of spontaneity—there seems to be here a kind of ontological priority of the in-itself over the for-itself. Therefore we must consider the previous remarks as simple attempts to clear the ground, and we must take up again from the beginning the question of facticity.

We have established that the for-itself is free. But this

does not mean that it is its own foundation. If to be free meant to be its own foundation, it would be necessary that freedom should decide the *existence* of its being. And this necessity can be understood in two ways. First, it would be necessary that freedom should decide its being-free; that is, not only that it should be a choice of an end, but that it should be a choice of itself as freedom. This would suppose therefore that the possibility of being-free and the possibility of not-being-free exist equally before the free choice of either one of them—*i.e.,* before the free choice of freedom. But since then a previous freedom would be necessary which would choose to be free—*i.e.,* basically, which would choose to be what it is already—we should be referred to infinity; for there would be need of another prior freedom in order to choose this and so on. In fact we are a freedom which chooses, but we do not choose to be free. We are condemned to freedom, as we said earlier, thrown into freedom or, as Heidegger says, "abandoned." And we can see that this abandonment has no other origin than the very existence of freedom. If, therefore, freedom is defined as the escape from the given, from fact, then there is a *fact* of escape from fact. This is the facticity of freedom.

But the fact that freedom is not its own foundation can be understood also in another way which will lead to identical conclusions. Actually if freedom decided the existence of its being, it would be necessary not only that my being not-free should be possible, but necessary as well that my absolute non-existence be possible. In other words, we have seen that in the initial project of freedom the end turns back upon causes in order to constitute them as such; but if freedom is to be its own foundation, then the end must in addition turn back on its existence and cause it to arise. We can see what would result from this: the for-itself would itself derive from nothingness in order to attain the end which it proposes to itself. This existence made legitimate by means of its end would be existence by *right* but not in *fact*. And it is true that among the thousands of ways which the for-itself has of trying to wrench itself away from its original contingency, there is one which consists in trying to make itself recognized by the Other as an existence by right. We insist on our individual rights only within the compass of a vast project which would tend to confer existence on us in terms of the function which we fulfill. This is the reason why man tries so often to identify himself with his function and seeks to see in himself only the "Presiding Judge of the Court of Appeal," the "Chief Treasurer and Paymaster" *etc*. Each of these functions has its existence justified by its end. To be identified with one of them is to take one's own existence as saved from contingency. But these efforts to escape original contingency succeed only in better establishing the existence of this contingency. Freedom can not determine its existence by the end which it posits. Of course it exists only by the choice which it makes of an end, but it is not master of the fact that *there is* freedom which makes known to itself what it is by means of its end. A freedom which would produce its own existence would lose its very meaning as freedom. Actually freedom is not a simple undetermined power. If it were, it would be nothingness or in-itself; and it is only by an aberrant synthesis of the in-itself and nothingness that one is able to conceive of freedom as a bare power pre-existing its choices. It determines itself by its very upsurge as a "doing." But as we have seen, *to do* supposes the nihilation of a given. One does something *with* or *to* something. Thus freedom is a lack of being in relation to a given being; it is not the upsurge of a full being. And if it is this hole of being, this nothingness of being as we have just said, it supposes *all being* in order to rise up in the heart of being as a hole. Therefore it could not determine its existence from the standpoint of nothingness, for all production from the standpoint of nothingness can be only being-in-itself. . . .

Thus freedom is a lesser being which supposes being in order to elude it. It is not free not to exist or not to be free. We are going to grasp immediately the connection of these two structures. In fact, as freedom is the escape from being, it could not produce itself laterally *alongside* being and in a project of "surveying;" one can not escape from a goal in which one is not imprisoned. A projection of the self on the margin of being can in no way constitute itself as the nihilation of this being. Freedom is the escape from an engagement in being; it is the nihilation of a being which it *is*. This does not mean that human-reality exists *first*, to be free *subsequently*. "Subsequently" and "first" are terms created by freedom itself. The upsurge of freedom is effected by the double nihilation of the *being which it is* and of the being in the midst of which it is. Naturally freedom is not this being in the sense of being-in-itself. But by freedom's illuminating insufficiencies in the light of the end of the chosen, *there is* this being which is its own. Freedom *has to be* behind itself this being which it has not chosen; and precisely to the extent that it turns back upon it in order to illuminate it, freedom causes this being which is its own to appear in relation with the *plenum* of being— that is, to exist in the midst of the world. We said that freedom is not free to be free and that it is not free not to exist. This is because the fact of not being able not to be free is the *facticity* of freedom, and the fact of not being able not to exist is its *contingency*. Contingency and facticity are really one; there is a being which freedom has to be in the form of *non-being* (that is, of nihilation). To exist as *the fact* of freedom or to have to be a being in the midst of the world are one and the same thing, and this means that freedom is originally *a relation to the given.*

But what is this relation to the given? Are we to understand by this that the given (the in-itself) conditions freedom? Let us look more closely. The given does not *cause* freedom (since it can produce only the given) nor is it the *reason* of freedom (since all "reason" comes into the world through freedom). Neither is it the *necessary condition* of freedom since we are on the level of pure contingency. Neither is it an *indispensable matter* on which freedom must exercise itself, for this would be to suppose that freedom exists ready-made as an Aristotelian form or as a Stoic Pneuma and that it looks for a matter to work in. The given in no way enters into the constitution of freedom since freedom is interiorized as the internal negation of the given. It is simply the pure contingency which freedom exerts by denying the given while making itself a choice; the given is the plenitude of being which freedom colors with insufficiency and with *négatité* by illuminating it with the light of an end which does not exist. The given is freedom itself in so far as freedom exists; and whatever it does, freedom can not escape its existence. The reader will have understood that this given is nothing other than the in-itself nihilated by the for-itself which has to be it, that the body as a point of view on the world, that the past as the *essence* which the for-itself was—that these are three designations for a single reality. By its nihilating withdrawal, freedom causes a whole system of relations to be established, from the point of view of the end, between *all* in-itselfs; that is, between the *plenum* of being which is revealed then as the *world* and the being which it has to be in the midst of this *plenum* and which is revealed as *one* being, as *one* "this" which it has to be.

Thus by its very projection toward an end, freedom constitutes as a being in the midst of the world a particular datum which it has to be. Freedom does not choose it, for this would be to choose its own existence; but by the choice which it makes of its end, freedom causes the *datum* to be revealed in this or that way, in this or that light in connection with the revelation of the world itself. Thus the very contingency of freedom and the world which surrounds the contingency with its own contingency will appear to freedom only in the light of the end which it has chosen; that is, not as brute existents but in the unity of the illumination of a single nihilation. And freedom would never be able to reapprehend this ensemble as a pure *datum,* for in that case it would be necessary that this freedom be outside of all choice and therefore that it should cease to be freedom. We shall use the term *situation* for the contingency of freedom in the *plenum* of being of the world inasmuch as this *datum,* which is there only *in order not to constrain* freedom, is revealed to this freedom only as *already illuminated* by the end which freedom chooses. Thus the *datum* never appears to the for-itself as a brute existent in-itself; it is discovered always *as a cause* since it is revealed only in the light of an end which illuminates it. Situation and motivation are really one. The for-itself discovers itself as engaged in being, hemmed in by being, threatened by being; it discovers the state of things which surrounds it as the cause for a reaction of defense or attack. But it can make this discovery only because it freely posits the end in relation to which the state of things is threatening or favorable.

These observations should show us that the *situation,* the common product of the contingency of the in-itself and of freedom, is an ambiguous phenomenon in which it is impossible for the for-itself to distinguish the contribution of freedom from that of the brute existent. In fact, just as freedom is the escape from a contingency which it has to be in order to escape it, so the situation is the free coordination and the free qualification of a brute given which does not allow itself to be qualified in any way at all. Here I am at the foot of this crag which appears to me as "not scalable." This means that the rock appears to me in the light of a projected scaling—a secondary project which finds its meaning in terms of an initial project which is my being-in-the-world. Thus the rock is carved out on the ground of the world by the effect of the initial choice of my freedom. But on the other hand, what my freedom can not determine is whether the rock "to be scaled" will or will not lend itself to scaling. This is part of the brute being of the rock. Nevertheless the rock can show its resistance to the scaling only if the rock is integrated by freedom in a "situation" of which the general theme is scaling. For the simple traveler who passes over this road and whose free project is a pure aesthetic ordering of the landscape, the crag is not revealed either as scalable or as not-scalable; it is manifested only as beautiful or ugly.

Thus it is impossible to determine in each particular case what comes from freedom and what comes from the brute being of the for-itself. The given in-itself as *resistance* or as *aid* is revealed only in the light of the projecting freedom. But the projecting freedom organizes an illumination such that the in-itself is revealed by it *as it is* (*i.e.*, resisting or favorable); but we must clearly understand that the resistance of the given is not directly admissible as an in-itself quality of the given but only as an indication—across a free illumination and a free refraction—of an inapprehensible *quid*. Therefore it is only in and through the free upsurge of a freedom that the world develops and reveals the resistance which can render the projected end unrealizable. Man encounters an obstacle only within the field of his freedom.

Better yet, it is impossible to decree *a priori* what comes from freedom in the character of this or that particular existent functioning as an obstacle. What is an obstacle for me may not be so for another. There is no obstacle in an absolute sense, but the obstacle reveals its coefficient of adversity across freely invented and freely acquired techniques. The obstacle reveals this coefficient also in terms of the value of the end posited by freedom. The rock will not be an obstacle if I wish at any cost to arrive at the top of the mountain. On the other hand, it will discourage me if I have freely fixed limits to my desire of making the projected climb. Thus the world by coefficients of adversity reveals to me the way in which I stand in relation to the ends which I assign myself, so that I can never know if it is giving me information about myself or about it. Furthermore the coefficient of adversity of the given is never a simple relation to my freedom as a pure nihilating thrust. It is a relation, illuminated by freedom, between the *datum* which is the cliff and the *datum* which my freedom has to be; that is, between the contingent which it is not and its pure facticity. If the desire to scale it is equal, the rock will be easy for one athletic climber but difficult for another, a novice, who is not well trained and who has a weak body. But the body in turn is revealed as well or poorly trained only in relation to a free choice. It is because I am there and because I have made of myself what I am that the rock develops in relation to my body a coefficient of adversity. For the lawyer who has remained in the city and who is pleading a case, whose body is hidden under his lawyer's robe, the rock is neither hard nor easy to climb; it is dissolved in the totality "world" without in any way emerging from it. And in one sense it is I who choose my body as weak by making it face the difficulties which I cause to be born (mountain climbing, cycling, sport). If I have not chosen to take part in sports, if I live in the city, and if I concern myself exclusively with business or intellectual work, then from this point of view my body will have no quality whatsoever.

Thus we begin to catch a glimpse of the paradox of freedom: there is freedom only in a *situation,* and there is a situation only through freedom. Human-reality everywhere encounters resistance and obstacles which it has not created, but these resistance and obstacles have meaning only in and through the free choice which human-reality *is.* But in order better to grasp the meaning of these remarks and to derive the advantages which they allow, it will be well at present to analyze in the light of them certain specific examples. What we have called the facticity of freedom is the given which it has to *be* and which it illuminates by its project. This given is manifested in several ways although within the absolute unity of a single illumination. It is *my place, my body, my past, my position* in so far as it is already determined by the indications of Others, finally my *fundamental relation to the Other.* We are going to examine successively and with specific examples these various structures of the situation. But we must never lose sight of the fact that no one of them is given alone and that when we consider one of them in isolation, we are restricted to making it appear on the synthetic ground of the others.

A. MY PLACE

My place is defined by the spatial order and by the particular nature of the "thises" which are revealed to me on the ground of the world. It is naturally the spot in which I "live" (my "country" with its sun, its climate, its resources, its hydrographic and orographic configuration). It is also more simply the arrangement and the order of the objects which at present appear to me (a table, beyond the table a window, to the left of the window a cabinet, to the right a chair, and beyond the window the street and the sea), which indicate me as the reason for their order. It is not possible for me not to have a place; otherwise my relation to the world would be a state of survey, and the world would no longer be manifested to me in any way at all—as we have seen earlier. Moreover, although this actual place can have been assigned to me by my freedom (I have "come" here), I have been able to occupy it only in connection with that which I occupied previously and by following paths marked out by the objects themselves. This previous place refers me to another, this to another, and so on to the *pure contingency of my place;* that is, to that place of mine which no longer refers to anything else which is a part of my experience: the place which is assigned to me by my birth. . . .

It is only in the act by which freedom has revealed facticity and apprehended it as *place* that this place thus defined is manifested as an *impediment* to my desires, an obstacle, *etc.* Otherwise how could it possibly be an obstacle? An obstacle to *what?* A compulsion *to do what?* The story is told of an emigrant who was going to leave France for Argentina after the failure of his political party: When someone remarked to him that Argentina was "very far away," he asked, "Far from what?" And it is very certain that if Argentina appears "far away" to those who live in France, it is so in relation to an implicit national project which valorizes their place as French. For the internationalist revolutionary, Argentina is a center of the world as is any other country. But if we have by a primary project first constituted French territory as our absolute place, and if some catastrophe forces us to go into exile, it is in relation to this initial project that Argentina will appear to us as

69

"very far away," as a "land of exile"; it is in relation to this project that we shall feel ourselves expatriated.

Thus our freedom itself creates the obstacles from which we suffer. It is freedom itself which by positing its end and by choosing this end as inaccessible or accessible with difficulty, causes our placing to appear to our projects as an insurmountable resistance or a resistance to be surmounted with difficulty. It is freedom again which establishes the spatial connections between objects as the first type of a relation of instrumentality, which decides on techniques permitting distances to be measured and cleared, and thus constitutes its own *restriction*. But to be precise, freedom can exist only as *restricted* since freedom is choice. Every choice, as we shall see, supposes elimination and selection; every choice is a choice of finitude. Thus freedom can be truly free only by constituting facticity as its own restriction. It would therefore be to no point to say that I *am not free* to go to New York because of the fact that I am a minor government official at Mont-de-Marsan. On the contrary, it is in relation to my project of going to New York that I am going to *situate* myself at Mont-de-Marsan. My placing in the world, the relation of Mont-de-Marsan to New York and to China would be altogether different if, for example, my project were to become a wealthy farmer at Mont-de-Marsan. In the first case Mont-de-Marsan appears on the ground of a world which maintains an organized connection with New York, Melbourne, and Shanghai; in the second it emerges on the ground of an undifferentiated world. As for the *real* importance of my project of going to New York, I alone decide it. It can be just a way of choosing myself as discontented with Mont-de-Marsan; and in this case everything is centered on Mont-de-Marsan; I simply make proof of the need of perpetually nihilating my place, of living in a perpetual withdrawal in relation to the city which I inhabit. It can also be a project in which I wholly engage myself. In the first case I shall apprehend my place as an insurmountable obstacle, and I shall have simply used an indirect means to define it indirectly in the world. In the second case, on the other hand, the obstacles will no longer exist; my place will be no longer a point of attachment but a point of departure, for in order *to go* to New York, some point of departure is necessary. Thus I shall apprehend myself at any moment whatsoever as engaged in the world at my contingent place. But it is precisely this engagement which gives meaning to my contingent place and which is my freedom. To be sure, in being born I *take a place,* but I am responsible for the place which I take. We can see clearly here the inextricable connection of freedom and facticity in the situation. Without facticity freedom would not exist— as a power of nihilation and of choice—and without freedom facticity would not be discovered and would have no meaning.

B. MY PAST

We have a past. Of course we have been able to establish that this past does not determine our acts as a prior phenomenon determines a consequent phenomenon; we have shown that the past is without force to constitute the present and to sketch out the future. Nevertheless the fact remains that the freedom which escapes toward the future can not give itself any past it likes according to its fancy; there are even more compelling reasons for the fact that it can not produce itself without a past. It has to be its own past, and this past is irremediable. It even seems at first glance that freedom can not modify its past in any way; the past is that which is out of reach and which haunts us at a distance without our even being able to turn back to face it in order to consider it.

If the past does not determine our actions, at least it is such that we can not take a new decision except *in terms of it*. If I have been trained at a naval academy, and if I have become an officer in the Navy, at each moment that I assume myself and consider myself, I am engaged; at the very instant when I apprehend myself, I am on watch on the bridge of the ship of which I am second in command. I can suddenly revolt against this fact, hand in my resignation, decide on suicide. These extreme measures are taken in connection with the past which is mine; if they aim at destroying it, this is because my past exists, and my most radical decisions can succeed only in taking a negative position with respect to my past. But basically this is to recognize the past's immense importance as a backdrop and a point of view. Every action designed to wrench me away from my past must first be conceived in terms of my particular past; that is, the action must before all recognize that it is born out of the particular past which it wishes to destroy. Our acts, says the proverb, follow after us. The past is present and melts insensibly into the present; it is the suit of clothes which I selected six months ago, the house which I have had built, the book which I began last winter, my wife, the promises which I have made to her, my children; all which I *am* I have to be in the mode of having-been. Thus the importance of the past can not be exaggerated since for me "Wesen ist was gewesen ist," essence is what has been. But we find here the paradox pointed out previously: I can not conceive of myself without a past; better yet, I can no longer *think* anything about myself since I think about what I *am* and since I am in the past; but on the other hand I am the being through whom the past comes to myself and to the world.

Let us examine this paradox more closely. Since freedom is choice, it is change. It is defined by the end which it projects; that is, by the future which it has to be. But precisely because the future is the *not-yet-existing-state of what is* it can be conceived only within a narrow connection with what is. It is not possible that what is should illuminate what is not yet, for what is is a *lack* and consequently can be known as such only in terms of that ¡which it lacks. The end illuminates what is. But to go looking for the end to-come in order by means of it to make known that-which-is, requires being already beyond what-is in a nihilating withdrawal which makes what-is appear clearly in the state of an isolated-system. What-is, therefore, takes on its meaning only when it is *surpassed* toward the future. Therefore what-is is the past. We see how the past as "that ¡which is to be changed" is indispensable to the choice of the future and how consequently no free surpassing can be effected except in terms of a past. . . .

But while freedom is the choice of an end in terms of the past, conversely the past is what it is only in relation to the end chosen. There is an unchangeable element in the past, (*e.g.,* I had whooping cough when I was five years old) and an element which is eminently variable (the meaning of the brute fact in relation to the totality of my being). But since, on the other hand, the meaning of the past fact penetrates it through and through (I can not "recall" my childhood whooping cough outside of a precise project which defines its meaning), it is finally impossible for me to distinguish the unchangeable brute existence from the variable meaning which it includes. To say, "I had whooping cough when I was four years old" supposes a thousand projects, in particular the adoption of the calendar as a system of reference for my individual existence (hence the adoption of an original position with regard to the social order) and a confident belief in the accounts which third persons give of my childhood, a belief which certainly goes along with a respect or an affection for my parents, a respect which shapes its meaning for me, *etc.* That brute fact itself *is,* but apart from the witness of others, its date, the technical name of the illness (an ensemble of meanings which depend on my projects) what can it *be?* Thus this brute existence, *although necessarily existent and unchangeable,* stands as the ideal end— beyond reach—of a systematic specification of all the meanings included in a memory. There is, of course, a "pure matter" of memory in the sense in which Bergson speaks of pure memory; but when it shows itself, it is always in and through a project which includes the appearance of this matter in its purity.

Now the meaning of the past is strictly dependent on my present project. This certainly does not mean that I can make the meaning of my previous acts vary in any way I please; quite the contrary, it means that the fundamental project which I am decides absolutely the meaning which the past which I have to be can have for me and for others. I alone in fact can decide at each moment the *bearing* of the past. I do not decide it by debating it, by deliberating it, by deliberating over it, and in each instance evaluating the importance of this or that prior event; but by projecting myself toward my ends, I preserve the past with me, and by action I *decide* its meaning. Who shall decide whether that mystic crisis in my fifteenth year "was" a pure accident of puberty or, on the contrary, the first sign of a future conversion? I myself, according to whether I shall decide—at twenty years of age, at thirty years—to be converted. The project of conversion by a single stroke confers on an adolescent crisis the value of a premonition which I had not taken seriously. Who shall decide whether the period which I spent in prison after a theft was fruitful or deplorable? I—according to whether I give up stealing or become hardened. Who can decide the educational value of a trip, the sincerity of a profession of love, the purity of a past intention, *etc.?* It is I, always I, according to the ends by which I illuminate these past events.

Thus all my past is there pressing, urgent, imperious, but its meanings and the orders which it gives me I choose by the very project of my end. Of course the engagements which I have undertaken weigh upon me. Of course the marriage I made earlier, the house I bought and furnished last year limit my possibilities and dictate my conduct; but precisely because my projects are such I reassume the marriage contract. In other words, precisely because I do not make of it a "marriage contract which is past, surpassed, dead" and because, on the contrary, my projects imply fidelity to the engagements undertaken or the decision to have an "honorable life" as a husband and a father, *etc.*, these projects necessarily come to illuminate the past marriage vow and to confer on it its always actual value. Thus the urgency of the past comes from the future. . . .

Thus we choose our past in the light of a certain end, but from then on it imposes itself upon us and devours us. This is not because this past has an existence *by itself* different from that which we have to be but simply because: (1) it is the actually revealed materialization of the end which we are; (2) it appears in the midst of the world for us and for others, is never alone but sinks into the universal past and thereby offers itself to the evaluation of others. Just as the geometrician is free to create a particular figure which pleases him but can not conceive of one which does not immediately enter into an infinity of relations with the infinity of other possible figures, so our free choice of ourselves by causing the upsurge of a certain evaluative order of our past, causes the appearance in the world of an infinity of relations of this past to the world and to the Other. And this infinity of relations is presented to us as an *infinity of conducts to be adopted* since it is in the future that we evaluate our past. We are *compelled* to adopt these conducts in so far as our past appears within the compass of our essential project. To will this project, in fact, is to will the past; and to will this past is to will to realize it by a thousand secondary behaviors. Logically the requirements of the past are hypothetical imperatives: "If you wish to have such and such a past, act in such and such a way." But as the first term is a concrete and categorical choice, the imperative also is transformed into a categorical imperative.

But since the force of compulsion in my past is borrowed from my free, reflecting choice and from the very power which this choice has given itself, it is impossible to determine *a priori* the compelling power of a past. It is not only its content and the order of this content which my free choice decides; it is also the adherence of my past to my actuality. If within a fundamental perspective which we do not yet have to determine, one of my principal projects is to *progress*—i.e., to be always at any cost a little further advanced along a certain path than I was yesterday or an hour earlier, this progressive project involves in relation to my past a series of "uprootings." The past—which now from the height of my progress I regard with a slightly scornful pity—is that which is strictly a *passive object* for moral evaluation and judgment. "How stupid I was then!" or "How wicked I was!" It exists only because I can dissociate myself from it. I no longer enter into it, nor do I any longer wish to enter into it. This is not, of course, because it ceases to exist, but it exists only as *that self which I no longer am*—i.e., that being which I have to *be as the self which I am no longer*. Its function is to be what I have chosen of myself in order to oppose myself to it, that which enables me to measure myself. Such a for-itself chooses itself therefore without solidarity with itself, which means not that it abolishes its past but that it posits its past as not to be associated with it, exactly so as to affirm its total freedom (that which is past is a certain kind of engagement with respect to the past and a certain kind of tradition). On the other hand, there are other for-itselfs whose project implies the rejection of time and a narrow solidarity with the past. In their desire to find a solid ground these latter have, by contrast, chosen the past as that which they *are,* everything else being only an indefinite and unworthy flight from tradition. They have chosen *at the start* the refusal of flight; that is, *the refusal to refuse.* The past consequently has the function of requiring of them a fidelity. Thus we shall see that the former persons admit scornfully and easily to a mistake which they have made whereas the very admission will be impossible for the others without their deliberately changing their fundamental project; the latter will then employ all the bad faith in the world and all the subterfuges which they can invent in order to avoid breaking that faith in "what is" which constitutes an essential structure of their project.

Thus like place, the past is integrated with the situation when the for-itself by its choice of the future confers on its past facticity a value, an hierarchical order, and an urgency in terms of which this facticity *motivates* the act and conduct of the for-itself.

C. MY ENVIRONMENT

My "environment" must not be confused with the place which I occupy and which we have already discussed. My environment is made up of the instrumental-things which surround me, including their peculiar coefficients of adversity and utility. Of course in occupying my place, I prepare the ground for the revelation of my environment, and by changing place—an operation, which, as we have seen, I freely realize—I provide the basis for the appearance of a new environment. But on the other hand the environment can change or be changed by others without my having any hand in the change. To be sure, Bergson has shown in *Matter* and *Memory* that a single modification of my place involves the total change of my environment while it would be necessary to imagine a total and simultaneous modification of all my environment in order to be able to speak of a modification of my place. Now this global change of the environment is inconceivable, but the fact remains that my field of action is perpetually traversed by the appearances and disappearances of objects with which I have nothing to do. In a general way the coefficient of adversity and utility of complexes does not depend solely on my place, but on the particular potentiality of the instruments. Thus as soon as I exist I am thrown into the midst of existences different from me which develop their potentialities around me, for and against me. For example, I wish to arrive on my bicycle as quickly as possible at the next town. This project involves my personal ends, the appreciation of my place and of the distance from my place to the town, and the free adaptation of means (efforts) to the end pursued. But I have a flat tire, the sun is too hot, the wind is blowing against me, *etc.,* all phenomena which I had not foreseen: these are the environment. Of course they manifest themselves in and through my principal project; it is through the project that the wind can appear as a head wind or as a "good" wind, through the project that the sun is revealed as a propitious or an inconvenient warmth. The synthetic organization of these perpetual "accidents" constitutes the unity of what the Germans call my *Umwelt,* and this *Umwelt* can be revealed only within the limits of a free project—*i.e.,* of the choice of the ends which I am. . . .

Every free project in projecting itself anticipates a margin of unpredictability due to the independence of things precisely because this independence is that in terms of which a freedom is constituted. As soon as I project going to the nearby village to find Pierre, the punctures, the "headwind," a thousand foreseeable and unforeseeable accidents are given in my very project and constitute its meaning. Thus the unexpected puncture which upsets my projects comes *to take its place* in a world pre-outlined by my choice, for I have never ceased, if I may say so, *to expect it as unexpected.* And even if my path has been interrupted by something which I should never have dreamed of—like a flood or a landslide —in a certain sense this unpredictability was foreseen. Just as the Romans reserved in their temple a place for unknown gods, so in my project a certain margin of indetermination was created "for the unpredictable," and this was done not because of experience with "hard blows" or an empirical prudence but by the very nature of my project. Thus in a certain way, we can say that human reality is surprised by nothing.

These observations allow us to bring to light a new characteristic of a free choice: every project of freedom is an *open project* and not a closed project. Although entirely individualized, it contains within it the possibility of its further modifications. Every project implies in its structure the comprehension of the *Selbständigkeit* of the things in the world. This perpetual foreseeing of the unforeseeable as the margin of indetermination of the project which I am enables us to understand how it is that an accident or a catastrophe, instead of surprising me by its unknown or its extraordinary quality, always overwhelms me by a certain quality which it has of "being already seen—already foreseen," by its very obviousness and a kind of fatalistic necessity, which we express by saying, "This was bound to happen." There is nothing which astonishes in the world,

nothing which surprises us without our determining ourselves to be surprised. The original theme of astonishment
is not that this or that particular thing exists within the
limits of the world but rather that there is a world in
general; that is, that I am thrown among a totality of existents thoroughly indifferent to me. This is because in
choosing an end, I choose to have relations with these
existents and because these existents have relations among
themselves. I choose that they should enter into combination
to make known to me what I am. Thus the adversity of
which things bear witness to me is pre-outlined by my freedom as one of its conditions, and it is on a freely projected
meaning of adversity in general that this or that complex
can manifest its individual coefficient of adversity.

Each time that there is a question of the situation it is
necessary to insist on the fact that the state of things described has a reverse side. Here also if freedom pre-outlines
adversity in general, then this is one way of sanctioning the
exteriority and indifference of the in-itself. Of course adversity comes to things through freedom, but this is in so far
as freedom illuminates its facticity as "being-in-the-midst-of-
an-in-itself-of-indifference." Freedom gives itself things as
adverse (*i.e.,* it confers on them a meaning which makes
them things), but it is by assuming the very given which
will be meaningful; that is, freedom assumes its exile in
the midst of an indifferent in-itself in order to surpass this
exile. Conversely, furthermore, the contingent given which
is assumed can support even this primary meaning which is
the support of all others, this "exile in the midst of indifference" only in and through a free assumption of the
for-itself.

Such, in fact, is the primitive structure of the situation;
it appears here in all its clarity. It is by its very surpassing
of the given toward its ends that freedom causes the given

to exist as *this* given here (previously there was neither *this* nor *that* nor *here*) and the given thus *designated* is not formed in any way whatsoever; it is a brute existent, assumed in order to be surpassed. But at the same time that freedom is a surpassing of *this given,* it chooses itself as *this* surpassing of the given. Freedom is not just any kind of surpassing of any kind of given. By assuming the brute given and by conferring meaning on it, freedom has suddenly chosen itself; its end is exactly *to change this given,* just as the given appears as this given in the light of the end chosen. Thus the upsurge of freedom is the crystallization of an end *across a given* and the revelation of a given *in the light of* an end; these two structures are simultaneous and inseparable. We shall see later in fact that the universal values of the chosen ends are disengaged only by analysis; every choice is the choice of a concrete change to be bestowed on a concrete given. Every situation is concrete.

Thus the adversity of things and their potentialities in general are illuminated by the end chosen. But there is an end only for a for-itself which assumes itself as abandoned in the midst of indifference. By this assumption it brings *nothing* new into this contingent, brute abandonment except for a *meaning.* It is responsible for the fact that henceforth *there is* an abandonment, that this abandonment is revealed as a situation.

The for-itself by its upsurge causes the in-itself to come into the world; still more generally, it is by means of nothingness that "there is" the in-itself—that is, things. We have seen also that the reality-in-itself is there at hand, with its *qualities,* without any distortion or adjunction. We are simply separated from it by the various type of nihilation which we instate by our very upsurge: world, space and time, potentialities. We have seen in particular that although we are surrounded by *presences* (this glass, this inkwell, this table, *etc.*), these presences are inapprehensible as such, for they release whatever it may be of them only after a gesture or an act projected by us—that is, in the future. At present we are able to understand the meaning of this state of things. We are separated from things by nothing *except by our freedom;* it is our freedom which is responsible for the fact that *there are* things with all their indifference, their unpredictability, and their adversity, and for the fact that we are inevitably separated from them; for it is on the ground of nihilation that they appear and that they are revealed as bound one to another. Thus the project of my freedom adds *nothing* to things: it causes *there to be* things; that is, precisely, realities provided with a coefficient of adversity and utilizable instrumentality. Freedom makes these things reveal themselves *in experience*—that is, raise themselves successively on the ground of the world in the course of a process of temporalization. Finally our freedom causes these things to manifest themselves as out of reach, independent, separated from me by the very nothingness which I secrete and which I am. It is because freedom is condemned to be free—*i.e.,* can not choose itself as freedom —that there are things; that is, a plenitude of contingency at the heart of which it is itself contingency. It is by the assumption of this contingency and by its surpassing that there can be at once a *choice* and an organization of things *in situation;* and it is the contingency of freedom and the contingency of the in-itself which are expressed *in situation* by the unpredictability and the adversity of the environment. Thus I am absolutely free and absolutely responsible for my situation. But I am never free except *in situation.*

D. MY FELLOWMAN

To live in a world haunted by my fellowman is not only

to be able to encounter the Other at every turn of the road; it is also to find myself engaged in a world in which instrumental-complexes can have a meaning which my free project has not first given to them. It means also that in the midst of this world *already* provided with meaning I meet with a meaning which is *mine* and which I have not given to myself, which I discover that I "possess already." Thus when we ask what the original and contingent fact of existing in a world in which "there are" also Others can mean for our situation, the problem thus formulated demands that we study successively three layers of reality which come into play so as to constitute my concrete situation: instruments which are *already* meaningful (a station, a railroad sign, a work of art, a mobilization notice), the meaning which I discover as *already mine* (my nationality, my race, my physical appearance), and finally the Other as a center of reference to which these meanings refer. . . .

There is no doubt that my belonging to an inhabited world has the value of a *fact*. It refers to the original fact of the Other's presence in the world, a fact which, as we have seen, can not be deduced from the ontological structure of the for-itself. And although this fact only makes our facticity more deep-rooted, it does not evolve from our facticity in so far as the latter expresses the necessity of the contingency of the for-itself. Rather we must say: the for-itself *exists in fact;* that is, its existence can not be identical with a reality engendered in conformity to a law, nor can it be identical with a free choice. And among the factual characteristics of this "facticity"—*i.e.,* among those which can neither be deduced nor proven but which simply "let themselves be seen"—there is one of these which we call the existence-in-the-world-in-the-presence-of-others. Whether this factual characteristic does or does not need to be recovered by my freedom in order to be efficacious in any manner whatsoever is what we shall discuss a little later. Yet the fact remains that on the level of techniques of appropriating the world, the very *fact* of the Other's existence results in the fact of the collective ownership of techniques. Therefore facticity is expressed on this level by the fact of my appearance in a world which is revealed to me only by collective and already constituted techniques which aim at making me apprehend the world in a form whose meaning has been defined outside of me. These techniques are going to determine my belonging to collectivities: to the *human race,* to the national collectivity, to the professional and to the family group. . . .

Now then we can see how my freedom in a way recovers its own limits, for I can grasp myself as limited by the Other only in so far as the Other exists for me, and I can make the Other exist for me only as a subjectivity recognized by my assuming my being-for-others. There is no circle here. By the free assumption of this being-alienated which I experience, I suddenly make the Other's transcendence exist for me as such. It is only by my recognizing the *freedom* of anti-Semites (whatever use they may make of it) and by my assuming this *being-a-Jew* that I am a Jew for them; it is only thus that being-a-Jew will appear as the external objective limit of the situation. If, on the contrary, it pleases me to consider the anti-Semites as pure *objects,* then my being-a-Jew disappears immediately to give place to the simple consciousness (of) being a free, unqualifiable transcendence. To recognize others and, if I am a Jew, to assume my being-a-Jew are one and the same. Thus the Other's freedom confers limits on my situation, but I can *experience* these limits only if I recover this being-for-others which I am and if I give to it a meaning in the light of the ends which I have chosen. Of course, this very assumption is *alienated;* it has its outside, but it is through this assumption that I can experience my being-outside as outside.

How then shall I experience the objective limits of my being: Jew, Aryan, ugly, handsome, kind, a civil servant, untouchable, *etc.*—when will speech have informed me as to which of these are *my* limits? It can not be in the way in which I intuitively *apprehend* the Other's beauty, ugliness, race, nor in the way in which I have a non-thetic consciousness (of) projecting myself toward this or that possibility. It is not that these objective characteristics must necessarily be *abstract;* some are abstract, others not. My beauty or my ugliness or the insignificance of my features are apprehended by the Other in their full concreteness, and it is this concreteness which the Other's speech will indicate to me; it is toward this that I shall emptily direct myself. Therefore we are not dealing with an abstraction but with an ensemble of structures, of which certain are abstract but whose totality is an absolute concrete, an ensemble which simply is indicated to me as on principle escaping me. This ensemble is in fact what I *am.* Now we observed at the beginning of Part Two that the for-itself can not *be* anything. For-myself I am not a professor or a waiter in a café, nor am I handsome or ugly, Jew or Aryan, spiritual, vulgar, or distinguished. We shall call these characteristics *unrealizables. . . .*

The fact that *there is* a beyond for life, a beyond which derives its meaning only through and in my life and which yet remains for me an unrealizable, and the fact that there is a freedom beyond my freedom, a situation beyond my situation and one for which what I live as a situation is given as an objective form in the midst of the world: here are two types of situation-limit which have the paradoxical character of limiting my freedom on every side and yet not having any other meaning than that which my freedom

85

confers on them. For class, for race, for the body, for the Other, for function, *etc.,* there is a "being-free-for—." By it the For-itself projects itself towards one of its possibles which is always its *ultimate possible,* for the envisaged possibility is a possibility of *seeing itself;* that is, of being another than itself in order to see itself from outside. In one case as in the other there is a projection of self towards an "ultimate" which thereby interiorized becomes a thematic out-of-reach meaning of hierarchized possibles. One can "be-in-order-to-be-French," "be-in-order-to-be-a-worker," the son of a king can "be-in-order-to-reign." We are dealing here with limits and negating *states* of our being which we have to assume in the sense in which, for example, the Zionist Jew resolutely assumes himself within his race—that is, assumes concretely and once and for all the permanent *alienation* of his being; in the same way the revolutionary worker by his very revolutionary project assumes a "being-in-order-to-be-a-worker." And we shall note as Heidegger did (although the expressions "authentic" and "unauthentic" which he employs are dubious and insincere because of their implicit moral content) that the attitude of refusal and of flight which remains always possible is despite itself the free assumption of what it is fleeing. Thus the bourgeois makes himself a bourgeois by denying that there are any classes, just as the worker makes himself a worker by asserting that classes exist and by realizing through his revolutionary activity his "being-in-a-class." But these external limits of freedom, precisely because they are external and are interiorized only as unrealizables, will never be either a *real* obstacle for freedom or a limit suffered. Freedom is total and infinite, which does not mean that it has no limits but that it *never encounters them.* The only limits which freedom bumps up against at each moment are those which it imposes on itself and of which we have spoken in connection with the past, with the environment, and with techniques.

E. MY DEATH

After death had appeared to us as pre-eminently non-human since it was what there was on the other side of the "wall," we decided suddenly to consider it from a wholly different point of view—that is, as an event of human life. This change is easily explained: death is a *boundary,* and every boundary (whether it be final or initial) is a *Janus bifrons.* Whether it is thought of as adhering to the nothingness of being which limits the process considered or whether on the contrary it is revealed as adhesive to the series which it terminates, in either case it is a being which belongs to an existent process and which in a certain way constitutes the meaning of the process. Thus the final chord of a melody always looks on the one side toward silence— that is, toward the nothingness of sound which will follow the melody; in one sense it is made with the silence since the silence which will follow is already present in the resolved chord as its meaning. But on the other side it adheres to this *plenum* of being which is the melody intended; without the chord this melody would remain in the air, and this final indecision would flow back from note to note to confer on each of them the quality of being unfinished.

Death has always been—rightly or wrongly is what we can not yet determine—considered as the final boundary of human life. As such it was natural that a philosophy which was primarily concerned to make precise the human position in relation to the non-human which surrounded it, would first consider death as a door opening upon the nothingness of human-reality, and that this nothingness would be the absolute cessation of being or else existence in a non-human form. Thus we may say that there has been—in correlation with the great realist theories—a realistic conception of death such that death appeared as an immediate contact with the non-human. Thus death escaped man at the same time that it rounded him off with the non-human absolute. It was not possible, of course, for an idealist and humanistic conception of the real to tolerate the idea that man would encounter the non-human even as his limit. It would then have sufficed in fact, to adopt the point of view of this limit in order to illuminate man with a non-human light. The idealist attempt to *recover* death was not originally the fact of philosophers but that of poets like Rilke or novelists like Malraux. It was sufficient to consider death as the final term *belonging to the series.* If the series thus recovers its *terminus ad quem,* then precisely because of this *ad* which indicates its interiority, death as the end of life is interiorized and humanized. Man can no longer encounter anything but the human; there is no longer any *other side* of life, and death is a human phenomenon; it is the final phenomenon of life and is still life. As such it influences the entire life by a reverse flow. Life is limited by life; it becomes like the world of Einstein, "finite but unlimited." Death becomes the meaning of life as the resolved chord is the meaning of the melody. There is nothing miraculous in this; it is one term in the series under consideration, and, as one knows, each term of a series is always present in all the terms of the series. . . .

Thus by admitting that my death can be revealed in my life, we see that it can not be a pure arresting of my subjectivity; for such an arresting, since it is an inner event of this subjectivity, could finally be concerned only with the subjectivity. If it is true that dogmatic realism was wrong in viewing death as *the state of death*—i.e., as a transcendent to life—the fact remains that death such that I can discover it as *mine* necessarily engages something other than myself. In fact in so far as it is the always possible nihilation of my possibles, it is outside my possibilities and therefore I can not wait for it; that is, I can not thrust myself toward it as towards one of my possibilities. Death can not therefore belong to the ontological structure of the for-itself. . . .

Death, far from being my peculiar possibility, is *a contingent fact* which as such on principle escapes me and originally belongs to my facticity. I can neither discover my death nor wait for it nor adopt an attitude toward it, for it is that which is revealed as undiscoverable, that which disarms all waiting, that which slips into all attitudes (and particularly into those which are assumed with respect to death) so as to transform them into externalized and fixed conducts whose meaning is forever entrusted to others and not to ourselves. Death is a pure fact as is birth; it comes to us from outside and it transforms us into the outside. At bottom it is in no way distinguished from birth, and it is the identity of birth and death that we call facticity. . . .

Thus death is in no way an ontological structure of my being, at least not in so far as my being is *for itself;* it is the *Other* who is mortal in his being. There is no place for death in being-for-itself; it can neither wait for death nor realize it nor project itself toward it; death is in no way the foundation of the finitude of the for-itself. In a general way death can neither be founded from within like the project of original freedom, nor can it be received from the outside as a quality by the for-itself. What then is death? Nothing but a certain aspect of facticity and of being-for-others—*i.e.,* nothing other than the *given.* It is absurd that we are born; it is absurd that we die. On the other hand, this absurdity is presented as the permanent alienation of my being-possibility which is no longer *my* possibility but that of the Other.

It is therefore an external and factual limit of my subjectivity!

But do we not recognize at this point the description which we attempted in the preceding section? This factual limit which on the one hand we must affirm since nothing penetrates us from outside and since in one sense it is very necessary that we *experience* death if we are to be able even to name it, this factual limit which, on the other hand, is never *encountered* by the for-itself since it does not enter into the for-itself save as the indefinite permanence of its being-for-others—what is this limit if not precisely one of the *unrealizables?* What is it if not a synthetic aspect of our *reverse side?* *Mortal* represents the present being which I am for the Other; *dead* represents the future meaning of my actual for-itself for the Other. We are dealing therefore with a permanent limit of my projects; and as such this limit is to be assumed. It is therefore an exteriority which remains exteriority even in and through the attempt of the for-itself to realize it. It is what we defined above as the *unrealizable to be realized.* There is basically no difference between the choice by which freedom assumes its death as the inapprehensible and inconceivable limit of its subjectivity and that by which it chooses to be a freedom limited by the fact of the Other's freedom. Thus death is not *my* possibility in the sense previously defined; it is a situation-limit as the chosen and fugitive reverse side of my choice. It is not *my* possible in the sense that it would be my own end which would make known to me my being. But due to the fact that it is an unavoidable necessity of existing elsewhere as an outside and an in-itself, it is interiorized as "ultimate;" that is, as a thematic meaning of the hierarchical possibles, a meaning out of reach.

Thus death haunts me at the very heart of each of my projects as their inevitable reverse side. But precisely because this "reverse" is to be assumed not as *my* possibility but as the possibility that there are for me no longer any possibilities, it does not penetrate me. The freedom which is *my freedom* remains total and infinite. Death is not an obstacle to my projects; it is only a destiny of these projects elsewhere. And this is not because death does not limit my freedom but because freedom never encounters this limit. I am not "free to die," but I am a free mortal. Since death escapes my projects because it is unrealizable, I myself escape death in my very project. Since death is always beyond my subjectivity, there is no place for it in my subjectivity. This subjectivity does not affirm itself *against* death but independently of it although this affirmation is immediately alienated. Therefore we can neither think of death nor wait for it nor arm ourselves against it; but also our projects as projects are independent of death—not because of our blindness, as the Christian says, but on principle. And although there are innumerable possible attitudes with which we may confront this unrealizable which "in the bargain" is to be realized, there is no place for classifying these attitudes as authentic or unauthentic since we always die *in the bargain.*

These various descriptions relating to my place, my past, my environment, my death, and my fellowman do not claim to be exhaustive or even detailed. Their aim is simply to grant us a clearer conception of the "situation." Thanks to these descriptions, it is going to be possible for us to define more precisely this "being-in-situation" which characterizes the For-itself in so far as it is responsible for its manner of being without being the foundation of its being. . . .

The situation can not be *subjective,* for it is neither the sum nor the unity of the *impressions* which things make on us. It is *the things themselves* and myself among things; for my upsurge into the world as the pure nihilation of being has no other result but to cause there to be things, and it adds *nothing*. In this aspect the situation betrays my *facticity;* that is, the fact that things simply *are there* as they are without the necessity or the possibility of being otherwise and that I *am there* among them.

But neither can the situation be *objective* in the sense that it would be a pure given which the subject would establish without being in any way engaged in the system thus constituted. In fact the situation by the very meaning of the given (a meaning without which there *would not even be* any given) reflects to the for-itself its freedom. If the situation is neither subjective nor objective, this is because it does not constitute a *knowledge* nor even an affective comprehension of the state of the world by a subject. The situation is a *relation of being* between a for-itself and the in-itself which the for-itself nihilates. The situation is the whole subject (he is *nothing but* his situation) and it is also the whole "thing" (*there is* never anything more than things). The situation is the subject illuminating things by his very surpassing, if you like; it is things referring to the subject his own image. It is the total facticity, the absolute contingency of the world, of my birth, of my place, of my past, of my environment, of the fact of my fellowman—and it is my freedom without limits as that which causes there to be for me a facticity. . . .

Internal upheavals of the situation because of autonomous changes in the environment are always to be anticipated. These changes can never *provoke* a change of my project, but on the foundation of my freedom they can effect a simplification or a complication of the situation. Consequently my initial project will be revealed to me with more or less simplicity. For a person is never either simple or complex; it is his situation which can be one or the other. In fact I am nothing but the project of myself beyond a determined situation, and this project *pre-outlines* me in terms of the concrete situation as in addition it illumines the situation in terms of my choice. If therefore the situation in its ensemble is simplified, even if landslides, cave-ins, erosions have imprinted upon it a well-marked aspect of heavier features with violent contrasts, I shall myself be simple, for my choice—the choice which I am—is an apprehension of *this situation here* and can only be simple. The birth of new complications will have the result of presenting me with a complicated situation beyond which I shall find myself complicated. This is something which everyone has been able to establish if he has observed with what almost animal simplicity prisoners of war react following the extreme simplification of their situation. This simplification can not modify the meaning of the project; but on the very foundation of my freedom it causes my environment to become condensed and uniform and to be constituted in and through a clearer, more brutal, and more condensed apprehension of the fundamental ends of the captive person. In short we are dealing with an internal metabolism, not with a global metamorphosis which would affect as well the *form* of the situation. These are, nevertheless, changes which I discover as changes "in my life"—that is, changes within the unitary compass of a single project.

3. *Freedom and Responsibility*

Although the considerations which are about to follow are of interest primarily to the ethicist, it may nevertheless be worthwhile after these descriptions and arguments to return to the freedom of the for-itself and to try to understand what the fact of this freedom represents for human destiny.

The essential consequence of our earlier remarks is that

man being condemned to be free carries the weight of the whole world on his shoulders; he is responsible for the world and for himself as a way of being. We are taking the word "responsibility" in its ordinary sense as "consciousness (of) being the incontestable author of an event or of an object." In this sense the responsibility of the for-itself is overwhelming since he is the one by whom it happens that *there is* a world; since he is also the one who makes himself be, then whatever may be the situation in which he finds himself, the for-itself must wholly assume this situation with its peculiar coefficient of adversity, even though it be insupportable. He must assume the situation with the proud consciousness of being the author of it, for the very worst disadvantages or the worst threats which can endanger my person have meaning only in and through my project; and it is on the ground of the engagement which I am that they appear. It is therefore senseless to think of complaining since nothing foreign has decided what we feel, what we live, or what we are.

Furthermore this absolute responsibility is not resignation; it is simply the logical requirement of the consequences of our freedom. What happens to me happens through me, and I can neither affect myself with it nor revolt against it nor resign myself to it. Moreover everything which happens to me is *mine*. By this we must understand first of all that I am always equal to what happens to me *qua* man, for what happens to a man through other men and through himself can be only human. The most terrible situations of war, the worst tortures do not create a non-human state of things; there is no non-human situation. It is only through fear, flight, and recourse to magical types of conduct that I shall decide on the non-human, but this decision is human, and I shall carry the entire responsibility for it. But in addition the situation is *mine* because it is the image of my free choice of myself, and everything which it presents to me is *mine* in that this represents me and symbolizes me. Is it not I who decide the coefficient of adversity in things and even their unpredictability by deciding myself?

Thus there are no *accidents* in a life; a community event which suddenly bursts forth and involves me in it does not come from the outside. If I am mobilized in a war, this war is *my* war; it is in my image and I deserve it. I deserve it first because I could always get out of it by suicide or by desertion; these ultimate possibles are those which must always be present for us when there is a question of envisaging a situation. For lack of getting out of it, I have *chosen* it. This can be due to inertia, to cowardice in the face of public opinion, or because I prefer certain other values to the value of the refusal to join in the war (the good opinion of my relatives, the honor of my family, *etc.*). Anyway you look at it, it is a matter of a choice. This choice will be repeated later on again and again without a break until the end of the war. Therefore we must agree with the statement by J. Romains, "In war there are no innocent victims." If therefore I have preferred war to death or to dishonor, everything takes place as if I bore the entire responsibility for this war. Of course others have declared it, and one might be tempted perhaps to consider me as a simple accomplice. But this notion of complicity has only a juridical sense, and it does not hold here. For it depended on me that for me and by me this war should not exist, and I have decided that it does exist. There was no compulsion here, for the compulsion could have got no hold on a freedom. I did not have any excuse; for as we have said repeatedly in this book, the peculiar character of human-reality is that it is without excuse. Therefore it remains for me only to lay claim to this war.

But in addition the war is *mine* because by the sole fact

95

that it arises in a situation which I cause to be and that I can discover it there only by engaging myself for or against it, I can no longer distinguish at present the choice which I make of myself from the choice which I make of the war. To live this war is to choose myself through it and to choose it through my choice of myself. There can be no question of considering it as "four years of vacation" or as a "reprieve," as a "recess," the essential part of responsibilities being elsewhere in my married, family, or professional life. In this war which I have chosen I choose myself from day to day, and I make it mine by making myself. If it is going to be four empty years, then it is I who bear the responsibility for this.

Finally, . . . each person is an absolute choice of self from the standpoint of a world of knowledges and of techniques which this choice both assumes and illumines; each person is an absolute upsurge at an absolute date and is perfectly unthinkable at another date. It is therefore a waste of time to ask what I should have been if this war had not broken out, for I have chosen myself as one of the possible meanings of the epoch which imperceptibly led to war. I am not distinct from this same epoch; I could not be transported to another epoch without contradiction. Thus I *am* this war which restricts and limits and makes comprehensible the period which preceded it. In this sense we may define more precisely the responsibility of the for-itself if to the earlier quoted statement, "There are no innocent victims," we add the words, "We have the war we deserve." Thus, totally free, undistinguishable from the period for which I have chosen to be the meaning, as profoundly responsible for the war as if I had myself declared it, unable to live without integrating it in *my* situation, engaging myself in it wholly and stamping it with my seal, I must be without remorse or regrets as I am without excuse; for from the instant of my upsurge into being, I carry the weight of the world by myself alone without anything or any person being able to lighten it.

Yet this responsibility is of a very particular type. Someone will say, "I did not ask to be born." This is a naive way of throwing greater emphasis on our facticity. I am responsible for everything, in fact, except for my very responsibility, for I am not the foundation of my being. Therefore everything takes place as if I were compelled to be responsible. I am *abandoned* in the world, not in the sense that I might remain abandoned and passive in a hostile universe like a board floating on the water, but rather in the sense that I find myself suddenly alone and without help, engaged in a world for which I bear the whole responsibility without being able, whatever I do, to tear myself away from this responsibility for an instant. For I am responsible for my very desire of fleeing responsibilities. To make myself passive in the world, to refuse to act upon things and upon Others is still to choose myself, and suicide is one mode among others of being-in-the-world. Yet I find an absolute rseponsibility for the fact that my facticity (here the fact of my birth) is directly inapprehensible and even inconceivable, for this fact of my birth never appears as a brute fact but always across a projective reconstruction of my for-itself. I am ashamed of being born or I am astonished at it or I rejoice over it, or in attempting to get rid of my life I affirm that I live and I assume this life as bad. Thus in a certain sense I *choose* being born. This choice itself is integrally affected with facticity since I am not able to choose, but this facticity in turn will appear only in so far as I surpass it toward my ends. Thus facticity is everywhere but inapprehensible; I never encounter anything except my responsibility. That is why I can not ask, "*Why* was I born?" or curse the day of my birth or declare that I did not ask to be born, for these various attitudes toward my birth—*i.e.*, toward the *fact* that I realize a presence in the world—are absolutely nothing else but ways of assuming this birth in full responsibility and of making it *mine.* Here again I encounter only myself and my projects so that finally my abandonment —*i.e.*, my facticity—consists simply in the fact that I am condemned to be wholly responsible for myself. I am the being which *is* in such a way that in its being its being is in question. And this "is" of my being *is* as present and inapprehensible.

Under these conditions since every event in the world can be revealed to me only as an *opportunity* (an opportunity made use of, lacked, neglected, *etc.*), or better yet since everything which happens to us can be considered as a *chance* (*i.e.*, can appear to us only as a way of realizing this being which is in question in our being) and since others as transcendences-transcended are themselves only *opportunities* and *chances,* the responsibility of the for-itself extends to the entire world as a peopled-world. It is precisely thus that the for-itself apprehends itself in anguish; that is, as a being which is neither the foundation of its own being nor of the Other's being nor of the in-itselfs which form the world, but a being which is compelled to decide the meaning of being—within it and everywhere outside of it. The one who realizes in anguish his condition as *being* thrown into a responsibility which extends to his very abandonment has no longer either remorse or regret or excuse; he is no longer anything but a freedom which perfectly reveals itself and whose being resides in this very revelation. . . .

FREEDOM FROM PERSECUTION:
ANTI-SEMITE AND JEW

What makes the Jew is his concrete situation; what unites him to other Jews is the identity of their situations. This quasi-historical body should not be considered a foreign element in society. On the contrary, it is necessary to it. If the Church tolerated its existence at a time when the Church was all-powerful, it was because it took on certain economic functions that made it indispensable. Today those functions are open to all, but that does not mean that the Jew, as a spiritual factor, makes no contribution to the peculiar nature and equilibrium of the French nation. We have described objectively, perhaps severely, the traits of the inauthentic Jew. There is not one of them that is opposed to his assimilation *as such* in the national society. On the contrary, his rationalism, his critical spirit, his dream of a contractual society and of universal brotherhood, his humanism—all these qualities make him an indispensable leaven in that society.

What we propose here is a concrete liberalism. By that we mean that all persons who through their work collaborate toward the greatness of a country have the full rights of citizens of that country. What gives them this right is not the possession of a problematical and abstract "human nature," but their active participation in the life of the society. This means, then, that the Jews—and likewise the

Arabs and the Negroes—from the moment that they are participants in the national enterprise, have a right in that enterprise; they are citizens. But they have these rights *as* Jews, Negroes, or Arabs—that is, as concrete persons. . . .

But concrete liberalism . . . is a goal; it is in danger of becoming no more than a mere ideal if we do not determine upon the means to attain it. . . . The Jewish problem is born of anti-Semitism; thus it is anti-Semitism that we must suppress in order to resolve the problem. The question therefore comes back to this: What shall we do about anti-Semitism?

Ordinary procedures, particularly propaganda and education, are by no means without importance. It is to be hoped that the child in school will receive an education that will permit him to avoid errors of passion; but the results of such education may have only an individual reference. Likewise, we should not be afraid to prohibit by basic law statements and acts that tend to bring discredit upon any category of Frenchman. But let us have no illusions about the effectiveness of these measures: laws have never embarrassed and will never embarrass the anti-Semite, who conceives of himself as belonging to a mystical society outside the bounds of legality. We may heap up decrees and interdictions, but they will always come from the legal France, and the anti-Semite pretends that he represents the real France.

Anti-Semitism is a conception of the Manichaean and primitive world in which hatred for the Jew arises as a great explanatory myth. . . . It is not a matter of an isolated opinion, but of the total choice that a man in a situation makes of himself and of the meaning of the universe. It is the expression of a certain ferocious and mystical sense of real property. If we wish to make such a choice impossible, it will not be enough to address ourselves by propaganda, education, and legal interdictions against the liberty of the anti-Semite.

Since he, like all men, exists as a free agent within a situation, it is his situation that must be modified from top to bottom. In short, if we can change the perspective of choice, then the choice itself will change. Thus we do not attack freedom, but bring it about that freedom decides on other bases, and in terms of other structures.

Political action can never be directed against the freedom of citizens; its very nature forbids it to be concerned with freedom except in a negative fashion, that is, in taking care not to infringe upon it. It acts only on situations. We have demonstrated that anti-Semitism is a passionate effort to realize a national union *against* the division of society into classes. It is an attempt to suppress the fragmentation of the community into groups hostile to one another by carrying common passions to such a temperature that they cause barriers to dissolve. Yet divisions continue to exist, since their economic and social causes have not been touched; an attempt is made to lump them all together into a single one —distinctions between rich and poor, between laboring and owning classes, between legal powers and occult powers, between city-dwellers and country-dwellers, etc., etc.— they are all summed up in the distinction between Jew and non-Jew. This means that anti-Semitism is a mythical, bourgeois representation of the class struggle, and that it could not exist in a classless society. Anti-Semitism manifests the *separation* of men and their isolation in the midst of the community, the conflict of interests and the crosscurrents of passions: it can exist only in a society where a rather loose solidarity unites strongly structured pluralities; it is a phenomenon of social pluralism. In a society whose members feel mutual bonds of solidarity, because they are all engaged in the same enterprise, there would be no place for it.

Finally, anti-Semitism indicates a certain mystical and participationist liaison of man with his "goals" which results from the present system of property. Again, anti-Semitism would have no existence in a society without classes and founded on collective ownership of the instruments of labor, one in which man, freed of his hallucinations inherited from an older world, would at long last throw himself wholeheartedly into *his* enterprise—which is to create the kingdom of man. Anti-Semitism would then be cut at its roots.

Thus the authentic Jew who thinks of himself as a Jew because the anti-Semite has put him in the situation of a Jew is not opposed to assimilation any more than the class-conscious worker is opposed to the liquidation of classes. On the contrary, it is an access of consciousness that will hasten the suppression of both the class struggle and racism. The authentic Jew simply renounces for *himself* an assimilation that is today impossible; he awaits the radical liquidation of anti-Semitism for his sons. The Jew of today is in full war. What is there to say except that the socialist revolution is necessary to and sufficient for the suppression of the anti-Semite? It is for the Jews *also* that we shall make the revolution.

And while we wait for it? After all, it is a lazy way out to place on a future revolution the burden of liquidating the Jewish question.

Anti-Semitism is a problem that affects us all directly; we are all bound to the Jew, because anti-Semitism leads straight to National Socialism. And if we do not respect the person of the Israelite, who will respect us? If we are conscious of these dangers, if we have lived in shame because of our involuntary complicity with the anti-Semites, who have made hangmen of us all, perhaps we shall begin to understand that we must fight for the Jew, no more and no less than for ourselves.

I am told that a Jewish league against anti-Semitism has just been reconstituted. I am delighted; that proves that the sense of authenticity is developing among the Jews. But can such a league be really effective? Many Jews, and some of the best among them, hesitate to participate because of a sort of modesty: "That's biting off too much," one of them said to me recently. And he added, rather clumsily but with undoubted sincerity and modesty: "Anti-Semitism and persecution are not important."

It is easy enough to understand this repugnance. But *we* who are not Jews, should we share it? Richard Wright, the Negro writer, said recently: "There is no Negro problem in the United States, there is only a White problem." In the same way, we must say that anti-Semitism is not a Jewish problem; it is *our* problem. Since we are not guilty and yet run the risk of being its victims—yes, we too —we must be very blind indeed not to see that it is our concern in the highest degree. It is not up to the Jews first of all to form a militant league against anti-Semitism; it is up to us.

It is evident that such a league will not end the problem. Yet if it spread out all over France, if it succeeded in getting official recognition from the state, if its existence brought into being in other countries similar leagues with which it could unite to form ultimately an international association, if it intervened successfully wherever injustices were called to its attention, if it acted through the press, through propaganda and education, it would attain a triple result: First, it would permit the adversaries of anti-Semitism to know their strength and to unite in an active group; second, it would rally many hesitating people, people who have no convictions on the Jewish question, for an organized group always exercises a considerable force of attraction; finally, to an adversary who is always ready to contrast the real country with the legal country, it would offer the sight of a concrete community engaged in a particular fight having nothing to do with universalist abstractions of legality. This would take away from the anti-Semite his favorite argument, which rests on the myth of the concrete. The cause of the Jews would be half won if only their friends brought to their defense a little of the passion and the perseverance their enemies use to bring them down.

In order to awaken this passion, what is needed is not to appeal to the generosity of the Aryans—with even the best of them, that virtue is in eclipse. What must be done is to point out to each one that the fate of the Jews is *his* fate. Not one Frenchman will be free so long as the Jews do not enjoy the fulness of their rights. Not one Frenchman will be secure so long as a single Jew—in France or *in the world at large*—can fear for his life.

FREEDOM TO WRITE: WHY DOES ONE WRITE?

Each one has his reasons: for one, art is a flight; for another, a means of conquering. But one can flee into a hermitage, into madness, into death. One can conquer by arms. Why does it have to be *writing*, why does one have to manage his escapes and conquests by *writing?* Because, behind the various aims of authors, there is a deeper and more immediate choice which is common to all of us. We shall try to elucidate this choice, and we shall see whether it is not in the name of this very choice of writing that the engagement of writers must be required.

Each of our perceptions is accompanied by the consciousness that human reality is a "revealer," that is, it is through human reality that "there is" being, or, to put it differently, that man is the means by which things are manifested. It is our presence in the world which multiplies relations. It is we who set up a relationship between this tree and that bit of sky. Thanks to us, that star which has been dead for millennia, that quarter moon, and that dark river are disclosed in the unity of a landscape. It is the speed of our auto and our airplane which organizes the great masses of the earth. With each of our acts, the world reveals to us a new face. But, if we know that we are directors of being, we also know that we are not its producers. If we turn away from this landscape, it will sink back into its dark permanence. At least, it will sink back; there is no one mad enough to think that it is going to be annihilated. It is we who shall be annihilated, and the earth will remain in its lethargy until another consciousness comes along to awaken it. Thus, to our inner certainty of being "revealers" is added that of being inessential in relation to the thing revealed.

One of the chief motives of artistic creation is certainly the need of feeling that we are essential in relationship to the world. If I fix on canvas or in writing a certain aspect of the fields or the sea or a look on someone's face which I have disclosed, I am conscious of having produced them by condensing relationships, by introducing order where there was none, by imposing the unity of mind on the diversity of things. That is, I feel myself essential in relation to my creation. But this time it is the created object which escapes me; I can not reveal and produce at the same time. The creation becomes inessential in relation to the creative activity. First of all, even if it appears to others as definitive, the created object always seems to us in a state of suspension; we can always change this line, that shade, that word. Thus, it never *forces itself*. A novice painter asked his teacher, "When should I consider my painting finished?" And the teacher answered, "When you can look at it in amazement and say to yourself '*I'm* the one who did *that*!'"

Which amounts to saying "never." For it is virtually considering one's work with someone else's eyes and revealing what one has created. But it is self-evident that we are proportionally less conscious of the thing produced and more conscious of our productive activity. When it is a matter of pottery or carpentry, we work according to traditional norms, with tools whose usage is codified; it is Heidegger's famous "they" who are working with our hands. In this case, the result can seem to us sufficiently strange to preserve its objectivity in our eyes. But if we ourselves produce the rules of production, the measures, the

106

criteria, and if our creative drive comes from the very depths of our heart, then we never find anything but ourselves in our work. It is we who have invented the laws by which we judge it. It is our history, our love, our gaiety that we recognize in it. Even if we should regard it without touching it any further, we never *receive* from it that gaiety or love. We put them into it. The results which we have obtained on canvas or paper never seem to us *objective*. We are too familiar with the processes of which they are the effects. These processes remain a subjective discovery; they are ourselves, our inspiration, our ruse, and when we seek to *perceive* our work, we create it again, we repeat mentally the operations which produced it; each of its aspects appears as a result. Thus, in the perception, the object is given as the essential thing and the subject as the inessential. The latter seeks essentially in the creation and obtains it, but then it is the object which becomes the inessential.

This dialectic is nowhere more apparent than in the art of writing, for the literary object is a peculiar top which exists only in movement. To make it come into view a concrete act called reading is necessary, and it lasts only as long as this act can last. Beyond that, there are only black marks on paper. Now, the writer can not read what he writes, whereas the shoemaker can put on the shoes he has just made if they are his size, and the architect can live in the house he has built. In reading, one foresees; one waits. He foresees the end of the sentence, the following sentence, the next page. He waits for them to confirm or disappoint his foresights. The reading is composed of a host of hypotheses, of dreams followed by awakenings, of hopes and deceptions. Readers are always ahead of the sentence they are reading in a merely probable future which partly collapses and partly comes together in proportion as they progress, which withdraws from one page to the next and forms the moving horizon of the literary object. Without waiting, without a future, without ignorance, there is no objectivity.

Now the operation of writing involves an implicit quasi-reading which makes real reading impossible. When the words form under his pen, the author doubtless sees them, but he does not see them as the reader does, since he knows them before writing them down. The function of his gaze is not to reveal, by stroking them, the sleeping words which are waiting to be read but to control the sketching of the signs. In short, it is a purely regulating mission, and the view before him reveals nothing except for slight slips of the pen. The writer neither foresees nor conjectures; he *projects*. It often happens that he awaits, as they say, the inspiration. But one does not wait for himself the way he waits for others. If he hesitates, he knows that the future is not made, that he himself is going to make it, and if he still does not know what is going to happen to his hero, that simply means that he has not thought about it, that he has not decided upon anything. The future is then a blank page, whereas the future of the reader is two hundred pages filled with words which separate him from the end. Thus, the writer meets everywhere only *his* knowledge, *his* will, *his* plans, in short, himself. He touches only his own subjectivity; the object he creates is out of reach; he does not create it *for himself*. If he rereads himself, it is already too late. The sentence will never quite be a thing in his eyes. He goes to the very limits of the subjective but without crossing it. He appreciates the effect of a touch, of an epigram, of a well-placed adjective, but it is the effect they will have on others. He can judge it, not feel it. Proust never discovered the homosexuality of Charlus, since he had decided upon it even before starting on his book. And if a day comes when the book takes on for its author a semblance of objectivity, it is that years have passed, that he has forgotten it, that its spirit is quite foreign to him, and doubtless he is no longer capable of writing it. This was the case with Rousseau when he reread the *Social Contract* at the end of his life.

Thus, it is not true that one writes for himself. That would be the worst blow. In projecting his emotions on paper, one barely manages to give them a languishing extension. The creative act is only an incomplete and abstract moment in the production of a work. If the author existed alone he would be able to write as much as he liked; the work as *object* would never see the light of day and he would either have to put down his pen or despair. But the operation of writing implies that of reading as its dialectical correlative and these two connected acts necessitate two distinct agents. It is the conjoint effort of author and reader which brings upon the scene that concrete and imaginary object which is the work of the mind. There is no art except for and by others.

Reading seems, in fact, to be the synthesis of perception and creation. It supposes the essentiality of both the subject and the object. The object is essential because it is stictly transcendent, because it imposes its own structures, and because one must wait for it and observe it; but the subject is also essential because it is required not only to disclose the object (that is, to make *there be* an object) but also so that this object might *be* (that is, to produce it). In a word, the reader is conscious of disclosing in creating, of creating by disclosing. In reality, it is not necessary to believe that reading is a mechanical operation and that signs make an impression upon him as light does on a photographic plate. If he is inattentive, tired, stupid, or thoughtless, most of the relations will escape him. He will never manage to "catch on" to the object (in the sense in which we see that fire "catches" or "doesn't catch"). He will draw some phrases out of the shadow, but they will seem to appear as random strokes. If he is at his best, he will project beyond the words a synthetic form, each phrase of which will be no more than a partial function: the "theme," the "subject," or the "meaning." Thus, from the very beginning, the meaning is no longer contained in the words, since it is he, on the contrary, who allows the signification of each of them to be understood; and the literary object, though realized *through* language. On the contrary, it is by nature a silence and an opponent of the word. In addition, the hundred thousand words aligned in a book can be read one by one so that the meaning of the work does not emerge. Nothing is accomplished if the reader does not put himself from the very beginning and almost without a guide at the height of this silence; if, in short, he does not invent it and does not then place there, and hold on to, the words and sentences which he awakens. And if I am told that it would be more fitting to call this operation a re-invention or a discovery, I shall answer that, first, such a re-invention would be as new and as original an act as the first invention. And, especially, when an object has never existed before, there can be no question of re-inventing it or discovering it. For if the silence about which I am speaking is really the goal at which the author is aiming, he has, at least, never been familiar with it; his silence is subjective and anterior to language. It is the absence of words, the undifferentiated and lived silence of inspiration, which the word will then particularize, whereas the silence produced by the reader is an object. And at the very interior of this object there are more silences which the author does not tell. It is a question of silences which are so particular that they could not retain any meaning outside of the object which the reading causes to appear. However, it is these which give it its density and its particular face.

To say that they are unexpressed is hardly the word; for they are precisely the inexpressible. And that is why one does not come upon them at any definite moment in the reading; they are everywhere and nowhere. The quality of the marvelous in *The Wanderer* (*Le Grand Meaulnes*), the grandiosity of *Armance,* the degree of realism and truth of Kafka's mythology, these are never given. The reader must invent them all in a continual exceeding of the written thing. To be sure, the author guides him, but all he does is guide him. The landmarks he sets up are separated by the void. The reader must unite them; he must go beyond them. In short, reading is directed creation.

On the one hand, the literary object has no other substance than the reader's subjectivity; Raskolnikov's waiting is *my* waiting which I lend him. Without this impatience of the reader he would remain only a collection of signs. His hatred of the police magistrate who questions him is my hatred which has been solicited and wheedled out of me by signs, and the police magistrate himself would not exist without the hatred I have for him via Raskolnikov. That is what animates him, it is his very flesh.

But on the other hand, the words are there like traps to arouse our feelings and to reflect them toward us. Each word is a path of transcendence; it shapes our feelings, names them, and attributes them to an imaginary personage who takes it upon himself to live them for us and who has no other substance than these borrowed passions; he confers objects, perspectives, and a horizon upon them.

Thus, for the reader, all is to do and all is already done; the work exists only at the exact level of his capacities; while he reads and creates, he knows that he can always go further in his reading, can always create more profoundly, and thus the work seems to him as inexhaustible and opaque as things. We would readily reconcile that "rational intuition" which Kant reserved to divine Reason with this absolute production of qualities, which, to the extent that they emanate from our subjectivity, congeal before our eyes into impermeable objectivities.

Since the creation can find its fulfillment only in reading, since the artist must entrust to another the job of carrying out what he has begun, since it is only through the consciousness of the reader that he can regard himself as essential to his work, all literary work is an appeal. To write is to make an appeal to the reader that he lead into objective existence the revelation which I have undertaken by means of language. And if it should be asked *to what* the writer is appealing, the answer is simple. As the sufficient reason for the appearance of the aesthetic object is never found either in the book (where we find merely solicitations to produce the object) or in the author's mind, and as his subjectivity, which he cannot get away from, cannot give a reason for the act of leading into objectivity, the appearance of the work of art is a new event which cannot *be explained* by anterior data. And since this directed creation is an absolute beginning, it is therefore brought about by the freedom of the reader, and by what is purest in that freedom. Thus, the writer appeals to the reader's freedom to collaborate in the production of his work.

It will doubtless be said that all tools address themselves to our freedom since they are the instruments of a possible action, and that the work of art is not unique in that. And it is true that the tool is the congealed outline of an operation. But it remains on the level of the hypothetical imperative. I may use a hammer to nail up a case or to hit my neighbor over the head. Insofar as I consider it in itself, it is not an appeal to my freedom; it does not put me face to face with it; rather, it aims at using it by substituting a set succession of traditional procedures for the free invention of means.

112

The book does not serve my freedom; it requires it. Indeed, one cannot address himself to freedom as such by means of constraint, fascination, or entreaties. There is only one way of attaining it; first, by recognizing it, then, having confidence in it, and finally, requiring of it an act, an act in its own name, that is, in the name of the confidence that one brings to it.

Thus, the book is not, like the tool, a means for any end whatever; the end to which it offers itself is the reader's freedom. And the Kantian expression "finality without end" seems to me quite inappropriate for designating the work of art. In fact, it implies that the aesthetic object presents only the appearance of a finality and is limited to soliciting the free and ordered play of the imagination. It forgets that the imagination of the spectator has not only a regulating function, but a constitutive one. It does not play; it is called upon to recompose the beautiful object beyond the traces left by the artist. The imagination can not revel in itself any more than can the other functions of the mind; it is always engaged in an enterprise. There would be finality without end if some object offered such a set ordering that it would lead us to suppose that it has one even though we can not ascribe one to it. By defining the beautiful in this way one can—and this is Kant's aim—liken the beauty of art to natural beauty, since a flower, for example, presents so much symmetry, such harmonious colors, and such regular curves, that one is immediately tempted to seek a finalist explanation for all these properties and to see them as just so many means at the disposal of an unknown end. But that is exactly the error. The beauty of nature is in no way comparable to that of art. The work of art *does not have* an end; there we agree with Kant. But the reason is that it is an end. The Kantian formula does not account for the appeal which resounds at the basis of each painting, each statute, each book. Kant believes that the work of art first exists as fact and that it is then seen. Whereas, it exists only if one *looks* at it and if it is first pure appeal, pure exigence to exist. It is not an instrument whose existence is manifest and whose end is undetermined. It presents itself as a task to be discharged; from the very beginning it places itself on the level of the categorical imperative. You are perfectly free to leave that book on the table. But if you open it, you assume responsibility for it. For freedom is not experienced by its enjoying its free subjective functioning, but in a creative act required by an imperative. This absolute end, this imperative which is transcendent yet acquiesced in, which freedom itself adopts as its own, is what we call a value. The work of art is a value because it is an appeal.

If I appeal to my reader so that we may carry the enterprise which I have begun to a successful conclusion, it is self-evident that I consider him as a pure freedom, as an unconditioned activity; thus, in no case can I address myself to his passivity, that is, try to *affect* him, to communicate to him, from the very first, emotions of fear, desire, or anger. There are, doubtless, authors who concern themselves solely with arousing these emotions because they are foreseeable, manageable, and because they have at their disposal sure-fire means for provoking them. But it is also true that they are reproached for this kind of thing, as Euripides has been since antiquity because he had children appear on the stage. Freedom is alienated in the state of passion; it is abruptly engaged in partial enterprises; it loses sight of its task which is to produce an absolute end. And the book is no longer anything but a means for feeding hate or desire. The writer should not seek to *overwhelm;* otherwise he is in contradiction with himself; if he wishes to *make demands* he must propose only the task to be fulfilled. Hence, the character of pure presentation which appears essential to the work of

114

art. The reader must be able to make a certain aesthetic withdrawal. This is what Gautier foolishly confused with "art for art's sake" and the Parnassians with the imperturbability of the artist. It is simply a matter of precaution, and Genet more justly calls it the author's politeness toward the reader. But that does not mean that the writer makes an appeal to some sort of abstract and conceptual freedom. One certainly creates the aesthetic object with feelings; if it is touching, it appears through our tears; if it is comic, it will be recognized by laughter. However, these feelings are of a particular kind. They have their origin in freedom; they are loaned. The belief which I accord the tale is freely assented to. It is a Passion, in the Christian sense of the word, that is, a freedom which resolutely puts itself into a state of passivity to obtain a certain transcendent effect by this sacrifice. The reader renders himself credulous; he descends into credulity which, though it ends by enclosing him like a dream, is at every moment conscious of being free. An effort is sometimes made to force the writer into this dilemma: "Either one believes in your story, and it is intolerable, or one does not believe in it, and it is ridiculous." But the argument is absurd because the characteristic of aesthetic consciousness is to be a belief by means of engagement, by oath, a belief sustained by fidelity to one's self and to the author, a perpetually renewed choice to believe. I can awaken at every moment, and I know it; but I do not want to; reading is a free dream. So that all feelings which are exacted on the basis of this imaginary belief are like particular modulations of my freedom. Far from absorbing or masking it, they are so many different ways it has chosen to reveal itself to itself. Raskolnikov, as I have said, would only be a shadow, without the mixture of repulsion and friendship which I feel for him and which makes him live. But, by a reversal which is the characteristic of the im-

aginary object, it is not his behavior which excites my indignation or esteem, but my indignation and esteem which
give consistency and objectivity to his behavior. Thus, the
reader's feelings are never dominated by the object, and as
no external reality can condition them, they have their
permanent source in freedom; that is, they are all generous
—for I call a feeling generous which has its origin and its
end in freedom. Thus, reading is an exercise in generosity,
and what the writer requires of the reader is not the applica-
tion of an abstract freedom but the gift of his whole person,
with his passions, his prepossessions, his sympathies, his
sexual temperament, and his scale of values. Only this
person will give himself generously; freedom goes through
and through him and comes to transform the darkest masses
of his sensibility. And as activity has rendered itself passive
in order for it better to create the object, vice-versa, passivity
becomes an act; the man who is reading has raised himself
to the highest degree. That is why we see people who are
known for their toughness shed tears at the recital of imaginary misfortunes; for the moment they have become
what they would have been if they had not spent their lives
hiding their freedom from themselves.

Thus, the author writes in order to address himself to
the freedom of readers, and he requires it in order to make
his work exist. But he does not stop there; he also requires
that they return this confidence which he has given them,
that they recognize his creative freedom, and that they in
turn solicit it by a symmetrical and inverse appeal. Here
there appears the other dialectical paradox of reading; the
more we experience our freedom the more we recognize
that of the other; the more he demands of us, the more we
demand of him.

When I am enchanted with a landscape, I know very well
that it is not I who create it, but I also know that without

me the relations which are established before my eyes among the trees, the foliage, the earth, and the grass would not exist at all. I know that I can give no reason for the appearance of finality which I discover in the assortment of hues and in the harmony of the forms and movements created by the wind. Yet, it exists; there it is before my eyes, and I can make *there be* being only if being already *is.* But even if I believe in God, I can not establish any passage, unless it be purely verbal, between the divine, universal solicitude and the particular spectacle which I am considering. To say that He made the landscape in order to charm me or that He made me the kind of person who is pleased by it is to take a question for an answer. Is the marriage of this blue and that green deliberate? How can I know? The idea of a universal providence is no guarantee of any particular intention, especially in the case under consideration, since the green of the grass is explained by biological laws, specific constants, and geographical determinism, while the reason for the blue of the water is accounted for by the depth of the river, the nature of the soil and the swiftness of the current. The assorting of the shades, if it is willed, can only be something *thrown into the bargain;* it is the meeting of two causal series, that is to say, at first sight, a fact of chance. At best, the finality remains problematic. All the relations we establish remain hypotheses; no end is proposed to us in the manner of an imperative, since none is expressly revealed as having been willed by a creator. Thus, our freedom is never *called forth* by natural beauty. Or rather, there is an appearance of order in the ensemble of the foliage, the forms, and the movements, hence, the illusion of a calling forth which seems to solicit this freedom and which disappears immediately when one regards it. Hardly have we begun to run our eyes over this arrangement, than the call disappears; we remain alone, free to tie up one color with another or with a third, to set up a relationship between the tree and the water or the tree and the sky, or the tree, the water and the sky. My freedom becomes caprice. To the extent that I establish new relationships, I remove myself further from the illusory objectivity which solicits me. I *muse* about certain motifs which are vaguely outlined by the things; the natural reality is no longer anything but a pretext for musing. Or, in that case, because I have deeply regretted that this arrangement which was momentarily perceived was not offered to me by somebody and consequently is not *real,* the result is that I fix my dream, that I transpose it to canvas or in writing. Thus, I interpose myself between the finality without end which appears in the natural spectacles and the gaze of other men. I transmit it to them. It becomes human by this transmission. Art here is a ceremony of the *gift* and the gift alone brings about the metamorphosis. It is something like the transmission of titles and powers in the matriarchate where the mother does not possess the names, but is the indispensable intermediary between uncle and nephew. Since I have captured this illusion in flight, since I lay it out for other men and have disengaged it and rethought it for them, they can consider it with confidence. It has become intentional. As for me, I remain, to be sure, at the border of the subjective and the objective without ever being able to contemplate the objective ordonnance which I transmit.

The reader, on the contrary, progresses in security. However far he may go, the author has gone farther. Whatever connections he may establish among the different parts of the book—among the chapters or the words—he has a guarantee, namely, that they have been expressly willed. As Descartes says, he can even pretend that there is a secret order among parts which seem to have no connection. The creator has preceded him along the way, and the most beautiful disorders are effects of art, that is, again order. Reading is induction, interpolation, extrapolation, and the basis of these activities rests on the reader's will, as for a long time it was believed that that of scientific induction rested on the divine will. A gentle force accompanies us and supports us from the first page to the last. That does not mean that we fathom the artist's intentions easily. They constitute, as we have said, the object of conjectures, and there is an *experience* of the reader; but these conjectures are supported by the great certainty we have that the beauties which appear in the book are never accidental. In nature, the tree and the sky harmonize only by chance; if, on the contrary, in the novel, the protagonists find themselves in a *certain* tower, in a *certain* prison, if they stroll in a *certain* garden, it is a matter both of the restitution of independent causal series (the character had a certain state of mind which was due to a succession of psychological and social events; on the other hand, he betook himself to a determined place and the layout of the city required him to cross a certain park) and of the expression of a deeper finality, for the park came into existence only *in order to* harmonize with a certain state of mind, to express it by means of things or to put it into relief by a vivid contrast, and the state of mind itself was conceived in connection with the landscape. Here it is causality which is appearance and which might be called "causality without cause," and it is the finality which is the profound reality. But if I can thus in all confidence put the order of ends under the order of causes, it is because by opening the book I am asserting that the object has its source in human freedom.

If I were to suspect the artist of having written out of passion and in passion, my confidence would immediately vanish, for it would serve no purpose to have supported the order of causes by the order of ends. The latter would be supported in its turn by a psychic causality and the work of art would end by re-entering the chain of determinism. Certainly I do not deny when I am reading that the author may be impassioned, nor even that he might have conceived the first plan of his work under the sway of passion. But his decision to write supposes that he withdraws somewhat from his feelings, in short, that he has transformed his emotions into free emotions as I do mine while reading him; that is, that he is in an attitude of generosity.

Thus, reading is a pact of generosity between author and reader. Each one trusts the other; each one counts on the other, demands of the other as much as he demands of himself. For this confidence is itself generosity. Nothing can force the author to believe that his reader will use his freedom; nothing can force the reader to believe that the author has used his. Both of them make a free decision. There is then established a dialectical going-and-coming; when I read, I make demands; if my demands are met, what I am then reading provokes me to demand more of the author, which means to demand of the author that he demand more of me. And, vice-versa, the author's demand is that I carry my demands to the highest pitch. Thus, my freedom, by revealing itself, reveals the freedom of the other.

It matters little whether the aesthetic object is the product of "realistic" art (or supposedly such) or "formal" art. At any rate, the natural relations are inverted; that tree on the first plane of the Cézanne painting first appears as the product of a causal chain. But the causality is an illusion; it will doubtless remain as a proposition as long as we look at the painting, but it will be supported by a deep finality; if the tree is placed in such a way, it is because the rest of the painting *requires* that this form and those colors be placed on the first plane. Thus, through the phenomenal causality, our gaze attains finality as the deep structure of the object, and, beyond finality, it attains human freedom as its source and original basis. Vermeer's realism is carried so far that at first it might be thought to be photographic. But if one considers the splendor of his texture, the pink and velvety glory of his little brick walls, the blue thickness of a branch of woodbine, the glazed darkness of his vestibules, the orange-colored flesh of his faces which are as polished as the stone of holy-water basins, one suddenly feels, in the pleasure that he experiences, that the finality is not so much in the forms of colors as in his material imagination. It is the very substance and temper of the things which here give the forms their reason for being. With this realist we are perhaps closest to absolute creation since it is in the very passivity of the matter that we meet the unfathomable freedom of man.

The work is never limited to the painted, sculpted, or narrated object. Just as one perceives things only against the background of the world, so the objects represented by art appear against the background of the universe. On the background of the adventures of Fabrice are the Italy of 1820, Austria, France, the sky and stars which the Abbé Blanis consults, and finally the whole earth. If the painter presents us with a field or a vase of flowers his paintings are windows which are open on the whole world. We follow the red path which is buried among the wheat much farther than Van Gogh has painted it, among other wheat fields, under other clouds, to the river which empties into the sea, and we extend to infinity, to the other end of the world, the deep finality which supports the existence of the field and the earth. So that, through the various objects which it produces or reproduces, the creative act aims at a total renewal of the world. Each painting, each book, is a recovery of the totality of being. Each of them presents this totality to the freedom of the spectator. For this is quite the final goal of art: to recover this world by giving it to be seen as it is, but as if it had its source in human freedom. But, since what the author creates takes on objective reality only in the eyes of the spectator, this recovery is consecrated by the ceremony of the spectacle—and particularly of reading. We are already in a better position to answer the question we raised a while ago: the writer chooses to appeal to the freedom of other men so that, by the reciprocal implications of their demands, they may re-adapt the totality of being to man and may again enclose the universe within man.

If we wish to go still further, we must bear in mind that the writer, like all other artists, aims at giving his reader a certain feeling that is customarily called aesthetic pleasure, and which I would very much rather call aesthetic joy, and that this feeling, when it appears, is a sign that the work is achieved. It is therefore fitting to examine it in the light of the preceding considerations. In effect, this joy, which is denied to the creator, insofar as he creates, becomes one with the aesthetic consciousness of the spectator, that is, in the case under consideration, of the reader. It is a complex feeling but one whose structures and condition are inseparable from one another. It is identical, at first, with the recognition of a transcendent and absolute end which, for a moment, suspends the utilitarian round of ends-means and means-ends, that is, of an appeal or, what amounts to the same thing, of a value. And the positional consciousness which I take of this value is necessarily accompanied by the non-positional consciousness of my freedom, since my freedom is manifested to itself by a transcendent exigency. The recognition of freedom by itself is joy, but this structure of non-thetical consciousness implies another: since, in effect, reading is creation, my freedom does not only appear to itself as pure autonomy but as creative activity, that is, it is not limited to giving itself its own law but perceives itself as being constitutive of the object. It is on this level that the phenomenon specifically is manifested, that is, a creation wherein the created object is given *as object* to its creator. It is the sole case in which the creator gets any enjoyment out of the object he creates. And the word enjoyment which is applied to the positional consciousness of the work read indicates sufficiently that we are in the presence of an essential structure of aesthetic joy. This positional enjoyment is accompanied by the non-positional consciousness of being essential in relation to an object perceived as essential. I shall call this aspect of aesthetic consciousness the feeling of security; it is this which stamps the strongest aesthetic emotions with a sovereign calm. It has its origin in the authentication of a strict harmony between subjectivity and objectivity. As, on the other hand, the aesthetic object is properly the world insofar as it is aimed at through the imaginary, aesthetic joy accompanies the positional consciousness that the world is a value, that is, a task proposed to human freedom. I shall call this the aesthetic modification of the human project, for, as usual, the world appears as the horizon of our situation, as the infinite distance which separates us from ourselves, as the synthetic totality of the given, as the undifferentiated ensemble of obstacles and implements—but never as a demand addressed to our freedom. Thus, aesthetic joy proceeds to this level of the consciousness which I take of recovering and internalizing that which is non-ego par excellence, since I transform the given into an imperative and the fact into a value. The world is *my task,* that is, the essential and freely accepted function of my freedom is to make that unique and absolute object which is the universe come into being in an unconditioned movement. And, thirdly, the preceding structures imply a pact between human freedoms, for, on the one hand, reading is a confident and exacting recognition of the freedom of the writer, and, on the other hand, aesthetic pleasure, as it is itself experienced in the form of a value, involves an absolute exigence in regard to others; every man, insofar as he is a freedom, feels the same pleasure in reading the same work. Thus, all mankind is present in its highest freedom; it sustains the being of a world which is both *its* world and the "external" world. In aesthetic joy the positional consciousness is an *image-making* consciousness of the world in its totality both as being and having to be, both as totally ours and totally foreign, and the more ours as it is the more foreign. The non-positional consciousness *really* envelops the harmonious totality of human freedoms insofar as it makes the object of a universal confidence and exigency.

To write is thus both to disclose the world and to offer it as a task to the generosity of the reader. It is to have recourse to the consciousness of others in order to make one's self be recognized as *essential* to the totality of being; it is to wish to live this essentiality by means of interposed persons; but, on the other hand, as the real world is revealed only by action, as one can feel himself in it only by exceeding it in order to change it, the novelist's universe would lack thickness if it were not discovered in a movement to transcend it. It has often been observed that an object in a story does not derive its density of existence from the number and length of the descriptions devoted to it, but from the complexity of its connections with the different characters. The more often the characters handle it, take it up, and put it down, in short, go beyond it toward their own ends, the more real will it appear. Thus, of the world of the novel, that is, the totality of men and things, we may say that in order for it to offer its maximum density the disclosure-creation by which the reader discovers it must

124

also be an imaginary engagement in the action; in other words, the more disposed one is to change it, the more alive it will be. The error of realism has been to believe that the real reveals itself to contemplation, and that consequently one could draw an impartial picture of it. How could that be possible, since the very perception is partial, since by itself the naming is already a modification of the object? And how could the writer, who wants himself to be essential to this universe, want to be essential to the injustice which this universe comprehends? Yet, he must be; but if he accepts being the creator of injustices, it is in a movement which goes beyond them toward their abolition. As for me who read, if I create and keep alive an unjust world, I can not help making myself responsible for it. And the author's whole art is bent on obliging me to *create* what he *discloses,* therefore to compromise myself. So both of us bear the responsibility for the universe. And precisely because this universe is supported by the joint effort of our two freedoms, and because the author, with me as medium, has attempted to integrate it into the human, it must appear truly *in itself,* in its very marrow, as being shot through and through with a freedom which has taken human freedom as its end, and if it is not really the city of ends that it ought to be, it must at least be a stage along the way; in a word, it must be a becoming and it must always be considered and presented not as a crushing mass which weighs us down, but from the point of view of its going beyond toward that city of ends. However bad and hopeless the humanity which it paints may be, the work must have an air of generosity. Not, of course, that this generosity is to be expressed by means of edifying discourses and virtuous characters; it must not even be premeditated, and it is quite true that fine sentiments do not make fine books. But it must be the very warp and woof of the book, the stuff out of which the people and things are cut; whatever the subject, a sort of essential lightness must appear everywhere and remind us that the work is never a natural datum, but an *exigence* and a *gift*. And if I am given this world with its injustices, it is not so that I might contemplate them coldly, but that I might animate them with my indignation, that I might disclose them and create them with their nature as injustices, that is, as abuses to be suppressed. Thus, the writer's universe will only reveal itself in all its depth to the examination, the admiration, and the indignation of the reader; and the generous love is a promise to maintain, and the generous indignation is a promise to change, and the admiration a promise to imitate; although literature is one thing and morality a quite different one, at the heart of the aesthetic imperative we discern the moral imperative. For, since the one who writes recognizes, by the very fact that he takes the trouble to write, the freedom of his readers, and since the one who reads, by the mere fact of his opening the book, recognizes the freedom of the writer, the work of art, from whichever side you approach it, is an act of confidence in the freedom of men. And since readers, like the author, recognize this freedom only to demand that it manifest itself, the work can be defined as an imaginary presentation of the world insofar as it demands human freedom. The result of which is that there is no "gloomy literature," since, however dark may be the colors in which one paints the world, he paints it only so that free men may feel their freedom as they face it. Thus, there are only good and bad novels. The bad novel aims to please by flattering, whereas the good one is an exigence and an act of faith. But above all, the unique point of view from which the author can present the world to those freedoms whose concurrence he wishes to bring about is that of a world to be impregnated always with more freedom. It would be inconceivable that this unleashing of generosity provoked by the writer could be used to authorize an injustice, and that the reader could enjoy his freedom while reading a work which approves or accepts or simply abstains from condemning the subjection of man by man. One can imagine a good novel being written by an American Negro even if hatred of the whites were spread all over it, because it is the freedom of his race that he demands through this hatred. And, as he invites me to assume the attitude of generosity, the moment I feel myself a pure freedom I can not bear to identify myself with a race of oppressors. Thus, I require of all freedoms that they demand the liberation of colored people against the white race and against myself insofar as I am a part of it, but nobody can suppose for a moment that it is possible to write a good novel in praise of anti-Semitism. For, the moment I feel that my freedom is indissolubly linked with that of all other men, it can not be demanded of me that I use it to approve the enslavement of a part of these men. Thus, whether he is an essayist, a pamphleteer, a satirist, or a novelist, whether he speaks only of individual passions or whether he attacks the social order, the writer, a free man addressing free men, has only one subject—freedom.

Hence, any attempt to enslave his readers threatens him in his very art. A blacksmith can be affected by fascism in his life as a man, but not necessarily in his craft; a writer will be affected in both, and even more in his craft than in his life. I have seen writers, who before the war, called for fascism with all their hearts, smitten with sterility at the very moment when the Nazis were loading them with honors. I am thinking of Drieu la Rochelle in particular; he was mistaken, but he was sincere. He proved it. He had agreed to direct a Nazi-inspired review. The first few months he reprimanded, rebuked, and lectured his countrymen. No one answered him because no one was free to do so. He became irritated; he no longer *felt* his readers. He became more insistent, but no sign appeared to prove that he had been understood. No sign of hatred, nor of anger either; nothing. He seemed disoriented, the victim of a growing distress. He complained bitterly to the Germans. His articles had been superb; they became shrill. The moment arrived when he struck his breast; no echo, except among the bought journalists whom he despised. He handed in his resignation, withdrew it, again spoke, still in the desert. Finally, he kept still, gagged by the silence of others. He had demanded the enslavement of others, but in his crazy mind he must have imagined that it was voluntary, that it was still free. It came; the man in him congratulated himself mightily, but the writer could not bear it. While this was going on, others, who, happily, were in the majority, understood that the freedom of writing implies the freedom of the citizen. One does not write for slaves. The art of prose is bound up with the only regime in which prose has meaning, democracy. When one is threatened, the other is too. And it is not enough to defend them with the pen. A day comes when the pen is forced to stop, and the writer must then take up arms. Thus, however you might have come to it, whatever the opinions you might have professed, literature throws you into battle. Writing is a certain way of wanting freedom; once you have begun, you are engaged, willy-nilly.

Engaged in what? Defending freedom? That's easy to say. Is it a matter of acting as guardian of ideal values like Brenda's clerk before the betrayal, or is it concrete, everyday freedom which must be protected by our taking sides in political and social struggles? The question is tied up with another one, one very simple in appearance but which nobody ever asks himself: "For whom does one write?"

FREEDOM TO DO EVIL: SAINT GENET

. . . Once upon a time, in Bohemia, there was a flourishing industry which seems to have fallen off. One would take children, slit their lips, compress their skulls and keep them in a box day and night to prevent them from growing. As a result of this and similar treatment, the children were turned into amusing monsters who brought in handsome profits. A more subtle process was used in the making of Genet, but the result is the same: they took a child and made a monster of him for reasons of social utility. If we want to find the real culprits in this affair, let us turn to the decent folk and ask them by what strange cruelty they made of a child their scapegoat.

Action, whatever it be, modifies that which is in the name of that which is not yet. Since it cannot be carried out without breaking up the old order, it is a permanent revolution. It demolishes in order to build and disassembles in order to reassemble. From morning to night we heap up shavings, ashes, scraps. All construction entails an at least equal amount of destruction. Our unstable societies fear lest a false movement cause them to lose their balance. They therefore ignore the negative moment of our activities. We must love without hating the enemy of what we love, must affirm without denying the contrary of what we affirm, must elect without spurning those we have not elected, must produce without consuming. We rapidly cart away the dead, we stealthily recover waste, every day we mask, in the name of cleaning up, the destruction of the day before. We conceal the pillaging of the planet. The fear of knocking down the edifice is so great that we even take from ourselves our power of creating: we say that man does not invent, that he discovers. We reduce the new to the old. Upkeep, maintenance, preservation, restoration, renewal—these are the actions that are permitted. They all fall under the heading of repetition. Everything is full, everything hangs together, everything is in order, everything has always existed, the world is a museum of which we are the curators. Nevertheless, spirit, as Hegel says, is anxiety. But this anxiety horrifies us. We must eliminate it and arrest spirit by ejecting its springwork of negativity. Unable to get rid of this malignant postulation completely, the right-thinking man castrates himself; he cuts the negative moment away from his freedom and casts out the bloody mess. Freedom is thus cut in two; each of its halves wilts away separately. One of them remains within us. It identifies forever Good with Being, hence with what already is. . . .

The other half of his freedom, though cut away from him and cast far off, does not, however, leave him undisturbed. Poor right-thinking man: he wanted, in the beginning, to concern himself only with the positive and with Being, to obey unerringly, to realize on his own little plot of ground a small, local end of history. But the fact is that history does not stop; Being is paralyzed, surrounded by Nonbeing; and, in addition, man, man himself, be he respectful or scoffing, insolent or servile, cannot affirm without denying. If he poses a limit, he does so necessarily in order to transgress it, for he cannot pose it without at the same time posing the unlimited. Does he mean to respect a social prohibition? By the same impulse his freedom suggests that he violate it, for to give oneself laws and to create the possibility of disobeying them come to the same thing. The right-thinking man shuts himself up in a voluntary prison and locks the doors, but his stubborn freedom makes him leave by the window. . . .

. . . Right-thinking people have developed the myth of Evil by depriving human freedom of its positive power and reducing it to its negativity alone. Hence, the evil man, who is negative in essence, is a man possessed whose density, whatever he may say, will always be to harm. He is free to do evil; for him the worst is always certain. Indeed, it is not sufficient that his conduct have harmful consequences for others or that it seem blame-worthy in the eyes of others. If Evil wants to become absolute, it must be an object of loathing to the one who commits it. If the evil man could be in harmony with himself, this harmony would have the appearance of Good, and if his behavior seemed tolerable to him, he would sin out of ignorance or precipitancy, but not out of malignancy. He must plunge into the worst and at the same time be dragged into it by a kind of inverted grace; he must plunge and resist simultaneously; he must want to stop and to be pushed even further; he must adhere unreservedly to his aim to harm and must thrust it aside as the effect of an abominable inclination. The evil man approves and loathes himself; he loathes himself for approving himself, he approves himself for loathing himself. His entire consciousness is darkness at the core of his translucidity. This secret hebetude of consciousness is otherness: self and other than self in the absolute identity of self. Evil, which is Being and Nonbeing, Absolute and Relative, Principle and Person, Self-Respect and Self-Hatred, is, in the last analysis, both Order and Disorder. It is Disorder on principle since all its efforts are aimed at destroying order; as

Claudel says: "It does not compromise." And yet, if it is to be effective, it must at least have power to destroy, that is, it must have a kind of order, a technique, traditions. It is thus a disorder of all orders, an order of all disorders. It is a corrosive acid, a torment, an explosive, it is radical dispersion. It changes the most indissoluble unity into multiplicity. But since it strews Discord everywhere, since it is the greatest common factor, it must be the secret and imperceptible unity of all multiplicity.

If that is what Evil is, a geometric locus of all contradictions, it stands to reason that no one would dream of indulging in it unreservedly: "No man does evil voluntarily." Of course. What would he gain by it? Evil is gratuitous. It is a luxury activity that requires and yields no profit. We are told that "crime doesn't pay," and that is so. Evil, like Good, requires that it be its own reward. If you steal, or even kill, in order to live, living is a good, you have reduced plunder and murder to the role of means. Evil is fatiguing, it requires an unmaintainable vigilance. Schiller, who was haunted by Kantian ethics, used to ask himself uneasily regarding each of his acts: "Have I probed my mind? Has a self-seeking motive escaped me?" Similarly, the evildoer should ask himself anxiously: "Have I really done Evil for Evil's sake? Have I not acted out of self-interest?" Furthermore, the evil action, even if performed for its own sake, should contain within itself—and should resolve—so many contradictions that it would require invention, inspiration, in a word, genius. It would thus be akin, as Genet often states, to a work of art. Better still, to poetry. The folk mind is clearly aware that evil is beyond its means. It has invented the myth of the man who sold his soul to the Devil. This future victim has not enough strength of soul to do evil *for Evil's* sake. He seeks his own advantage, his pleasure, he wants gold, women, power. And it is Satan who, through him, engages in destroying souls out of pure and gratuitous malignity. At the end of a lecture in which I had attempted to expound the views of some contemporary moralists in all their complexity, a bright-eyed minister came up to me and said: "It's so much easier to do one's duty:" I must add that he corrected himself almost immediately. "And harder, too," he added. But I had understood his first reaction. Yes, Good, as they understand it, is easier than Evil. It is easy and reassuring "to do one's duty." It is a matter of training, since everything is repetition. Who would deliberately withdraw from the flock and its comfortable precepts to take up with that mutilated freedom whose bleeding stumps are writhing in the dust?

The conclusion that seems to follow is that the evildoer does not exist. It is only the Good man who is constantly preoccupied with Evil, since Evil is first his own freedom, that is, an enemy who is constantly springing up and whom he must constantly down. But let us not jump to conclusions. The evildoer does exist; we encounter him everywhere, at all times. He exists because the Good man invented him.

When King Louis XVI was brought back from Varennes, the bourgeois deputies realized with terror that all they had to do to become republicans was to carry their principles a bit further. Everything—their interests, their conservatism, their contempt for the masses—contributed to inspiring them with horror of a republic, and yet the idea was present, silent, passive, vertiginous. Their own freedom presented it to them as the logical consequence of their earlier act. Were they going to loathe themselves? Fortunately other citizens called for a republic. The Club des Cordeliers circulated a petition demanding that the King be deposed. What a relief! The possibility which

133

they feared now became quite foreign to them. It was still supported by a freedom, but this time it was a totally *other* freedom. It was as if this importunate part of their free will had actually withdrawn from them and gone off to lead an independent existence elsewhere. Supported by others, the idea of a republic ceased to be a temptation and became an object of horror. The petitioners were *evildoers,* and they were told as much. And whom does one strike in the person of the "dirty, greedy, sensual, negating" Jew? One's self, one's own greed, one's own lechery. Whom does one lynch in the American South for raping a white woman? A Negro? No. Again one's self. Evil is a projection. I would go as far as to say that it is both the basis and aim of all projective activity. As for the evildoer, we all have our own: he is a man whose situation makes it possible for him to present to us in broad daylight and in objective form the obscure temptations of our freedom. If you want to know a decent man, look for the vices he hates most in others. You will have the lines of force of his fears and terrors, you will breathe the odor that befouls his beauteous soul. In the case of those who condemn Genet most severely, I would say that homosexuality is their constant and constantly rejected temptation, the object of their innermost hatred, and that they are glad to hate it in another person because they thus have an opportunity to look away from themselves. And I do not mean, to be sure, that this constantly rejected homosexuality seems to them an inclination of their nature. Quite the contrary, it is diffuse, it is a shifty something about persons and things, it is a certain disturbing appearance of the world that might very well open up suddenly and become dizzying, it is an inner uneasiness, it is the dim and constant consciousness that there is no recourse within themselves against themselves. Genet is useful to them; they can hate in him the half of themselves which they reject.

Thus, the evildoer is the Other. Evil—fleeting, artful, marginal Evil—can be seen only out of the corner of one's eye and in others. Never is it more perceptible than in wartime. We know the enemy only by comparison with ourselves; we imagine his intentions according to ours; we set traps for him into which we know we would fall if we were in his place and we avoid those which we would have set. The enemy is our twin brother, our image in the mirror. Yet the same conduct which we consider good when it is ours seems to us detestable when it is his. He is the evildoer par excellence. It is therefore during a war that a Good man has the clearest conscience. It is in time of war that there are the fewest lunatics. Unfortunately, one cannot always be fighting. From time to time there must be peace. For peacetime, society has, in its wisdom, created what might be called professional evil-doers. These evil men are as necessary to good men as whores are to decent women. They are fixation abscesses. For a single sadist there is any number of appeased, clari-fied, relaxed consciousness. They are therefore very care-fully recruited. They must be bad by birth and without hope of change. That is why one chooses men with whom the decent members of the community have no reciprocal relationship: so that these bad people cannot take it into their heads to pay us back in kind and start thinking of us what we think of them. And as Evil is negation, separa-tion, disintegration, its natural representatives will be sought among the separated and separatists, among the unassimilable, the undesirable, the repressed, the rejected. The candidates include the oppressed and exploited in every category, the foreign workers, the national and ethnic minorities. But these are still not the best recruits.

These people sometimes organize among themselves, educate themselves and become conscious of their race or class. They then discover, through hatred, the meaning of reciprocity, and the oppressor comes to personify Evil for them just as they personify Evil for the oppressor. Fortunately there exist in our society products of disassimilation, castoffs: abandoned children, "the poor," bourgeois who lost their status, "lumpen-proletariat," déclassés of all kinds, in short, all the wretched. With these we are tranquil. They cannot unite with any group since nobody wants them. And as solitude is their lot, we do not have to worry about their associating among themselves. That is why, in general, we give them preference.

Genet fulfills all the required conditions. This abandoned child is an authentic castoff. He seems overwhelmed by a fabulous bad luck that guarantees us against any accidental return of reciprocity. Placed under observation for a time, he gave evidence of evil instincts and committed punishable offenses. This is all that was needed. By the gaze that surprised him, by the finger that pointed at him, by the voice that called him a thief, the collectivity doomed him to Evil. They were waiting for him. There was going to be a vacancy: some old convict lay dying on Devil's Island; there has to be new blood among the wicked too. Thus, all the rungs of the ladder which he has to descend have been prepared in advance. Even before he emerged from his mother's womb, they had already reserved beds for him in all the prisons of Europe and places for him in all shipments of criminals. He had only to go to the trouble of being born; the gentle, inexorable hands of the Law will conduct him from the National Foundling Society to the penal colony. . . .

FREEDOM FROM EXPLOITATION: THE
COLONIZER AND THE COLONIZED

Only the Southerner is competent to discuss slavery, because he alone knows the Negro; the puritanical and
abstract Northerners know man only as an entity. This fine
line of reasoning still has its uses: in Houston, in the
newspapers of New Orleans, and in "French" Algeria—
since we too are someone's Northerners. The newspapers
there tell us that the colonizer alone is qualified to speak
of the colony. The rest of us, who live in the mother
country, do not have this experience, so we are to view the
burning land of Africa through his eyes, which will just
show us the smoke.

For those intimidated by this criminal line of reasoning, I
recommend the reading of *The Colonizer and the Colonized*. Here, experience is matched against experience.
The author, a Tunisian, told of his bitter youth in *The
Pillar of Salt*. Exactly who is he? Colonizer or colonized?
He would say "neither"; you, perhaps, would say "both"
—it amounts to the same thing. He belongs to one of
those native but non-Moslem groups that are "more or
less privileged in comparison with the colonized masses,
but . . . rejected . . . by the colonizing group," which,
however, "does not completely discourage" their efforts
to integrate themselves into European society. Linked by
actual liabilities to the subproletariat, but separated from

137

it by meager privileges, the members of this group live in a constant state of uneasiness. Memmi himself has experienced a twofold liability, a twofold rejection, in the process that sets colonizers against "self-accepting colonizers." He has understood the system so well because he felt it first as his own contradiction. He explains very clearly in the book that such rendings of the spirit, plainly introjections of social conflicts, do not dispose the individual to action. But the man who suffers them, if he becomes aware of himself, can enlighten others through his self-examination: a "negligible force in the confrontation," he *represents* no one, but since he *is* everyone at once, he will prove to be the best of witnesses.

But Memmi's book is not a chronicle. The author may feed on memories, but he has assimilated them all. The book is rather the *formulation* of an experience: caught between the racist usurpation of the colonizers and the building of a future nation by the colonified, where the author "suspects he will have no place," he attempts to live his particularity by transcending it in the direction of the universal. The transcendence is not toward Man, who does not yet exist, but toward a rigorous reason enforcing its claims on everyone. This lucid and sober work may be classed among the "passionate geometries," for its calm objectivity represents transcendence of suffering and anger.

This is doubtless the reason Memmi might be reproached for his seeming idealism; in fact, he tells all. But one can haggle with him about his method. Perhaps it would have been better to show the colonizer and his victim both throttled, but the colonial *apparatus,* that cumbersome machine, constructed at the close of the Second Empire and under the Third Republic, that now, after giving the colonizers every satisfaction, turns against them and threatens to crush them. In fact, racism is built into the system: the colony sells produce and raw materials cheaply, and purchases manufactured goods at very high prices from the mother country. This singular trade is profitable to both parties only if the native works for little or nothing. The colonial agricultural subproletariat cannot even count on an alliance with the least-favored Europeans, for everyone lives off them, even the "small colonizers," whom the big proprietors exploit, but who are privileged compared to the Algerians, the average income of the Algerian Frenchman being ten times that of the Algerian Moslem. Here the tension is born. To keep salaries and the cost of living at a minimum, there must be great competition among native workers, so the birth rate must rise; but since the country's resources are earmarked for colonialist appropriation, the Moslem standard of living, on constant wages, continues to fall. The population thus lives in a chronic state of malnutrition. Conquest occurred through violence, and over-exploitation and oppression necessitate continued violence, so the army is present. There would be no contradiction in that, if terror reigned everywhere in the world, but the colonizer enjoys, in the mother country, democratic rights that the colonialist system refuses to the colonized native. In fact, the colonialist system favors population growth to reduce the cost of labor, and it forbids assimilation of the natives, whose numerical super-Colonialism denies human rights to human beings whom it has subdued by violence and keeps them by force in a state of misery and ignorance that Marx would rightly call a subhuman condition. Racism is ingrained in actions, institutions and in the nature of the colonialist methods of production and exchange. Political and social regulations reinforce one another. Since the native is subhuman, the Declaration of Human Rights does not apply to him; inversely, since he has no rights, he is abandoned without protection to inhuman forces—brought in with the colonialist praxis, en-

139

gendered every moment by the colonialist apparatus, and sustained by relations of production that define two sorts of individuals—one for whom privilege and humanity are one, who becomes a human being through exercising his rights; and the other, for whom a denial of rights sanctions misery, chronic hunger, ignorance, or, in general, "subhumanity." I have always thought that ideas take form from things and and that the ideas are already within man when he awakens them and expresses them to elucidate his situation. The colonizer's "conservatism" and "racism," his ambiguous relations with the mother country—such things are given *first,* before he revives them into Negro complexes.

Memmi would no doubt reply that he is saying nothing else. I know that. (Does he not say, "The colonial situation manufactures colonizers as it manufactures colonies?" The whole difference between us arises perhaps because he sees a situation where I see a system.) Moreover, perhaps it is Memmi who is right in expressing his ideas in the order of discovery; that is, starting with human intentions and felt relationships, he guarantees the genuineness of his experience. He suffered first in his relations with others and in his relations with himself; he encountered the objective structure in thoroughly studying the contradiction that was rending him, and he delivers structure and contradiction up to us just as they are, raw and still permeated with his subjectivity.

Let us stop haggling. The work establishes some strong truths. First of all, that there are neither good nor bad colonists: there are colonialists. Among these, some reject their objective reality. Borne along by the colonialist apparatus, they do every day in reality what they condemn in fantasy, for all their actions contribute to the maintenance of oppression. They will change nothing and will serve no one, but will succeed only in finding moral comfort in malaise.

140

The others—by far the greater number—sooner or later accept themselves.

Memmi has strikingly described the sequence of steps that leads them to "self-absolution." Conservatism brings about the selection of mediocre men. How can an elite of usurpers, aware of their mediocrity, establish their privileges? By one means only: debasing the colonized to exalt themselves, denying the title of humanity to the natives, and defining them as simply absences of qualities—animals, not humans. This does not prove hard to do, for the system deprives them of everything. Colonialist practice has engraved the colonialist idea into things themselves; it is the movement of things that designates colonizer and colonialized alike. Thus oppression justifies itself through oppression: the oppressors produce and maintain by force the evils that render the oppressed, in their eyes, more and more like what they would have to be like to deserve their fate. The colonizer can only exonerate himself in the systematic pursuit of the "dehumanization" of the colonized by identifying himself a little more each day with the colonialist apparatus. Terror and exploitation dehumanize, and the exploiter authorizes himself with that dehumanization to carry his exploitation further. The engine of colonialism turns in a circle; it is impossible to distinguish between its praxis and objective necessity. Moments of colonialism, they sometimes condition one another and sometimes blend. Oppression means, first of all, the oppressor's hatred for the oppressed. There exists a solitary limit to this venture of destructiveness, and that is colonialism itself. Here the colonizer encounters a contradiction of his own: "Were the colonized to disappear, so would colonization—with the colonizer." There would be no more subproletariat, no more over-eploitation. The usual forms of capitalist exploitation would reassert themselves, and prices and wages would fall into line with those of the mother country. This would spell ruin. The system wills simultaneously the death and the multiplication of its victims. Any transformation would be fatal to the system. Whether the colonized are assimilated or massacred, the cost of labor will rise. The onerous engine suspends between life and death, and always closer to death, those who are compelled to drive it. A petrified ideology devotes itself to regarding human beings as talking beasts. But it does so in vain, for the colonizers must recognize them first, even to give them the harshest or most insulting of orders. And since the colonizers cannot constantly supervise the colonized, the colonizers must resolve to trust them. No one can treat a man like a dog without first regarding him as a man. The impossible dehumanization of the oppressed, on the other side of the coin, becomes the alienation of the oppressor. It is the oppressor himself who restores, with his slightest gesture, the humanity he seeks to destroy; and, since he denies humanity in others, he regards it everywhere as his enemy. To handle this, the colonizer must assume the opaque rigidity and imperviousness of stone. In short, he must dehumanize himself, as well.

A relentless reciprocity binds the colonizer to the colonized—his product and his fate. Memmi has vividly recorded this. With him, we find that the colonialist system is a form in motion, born towards the middle of the last century, that will manufacture its own destruction of itself. For a long time now, colonialism has cost mother countries more than it has earned. France is crushed under the burden of Algeria, and we now know that we shall abandon the war, without victory or defeat, when we are too poor to pay for it. It is above all the rigidity of the colonialist apparatus that is causing its breakdown. The old social structures are pulverized, the natives are "atomized"—and colonialist society cannot integrate them without destroying itself. Thus the

142

colonized must rediscover their unity in opposition to that society. The excluded human beings will affirm their exclusivity in national selfhood. Colonialism creates the patriotism of the colonized. Kept at the level of a beast by an oppressive system, the natives are given no rights, not even the right to live. Their condition worsens daily. And when a people has no choice but how it will die; when a people has received from its oppressors only the gift of despair, what does it have to lose? A people's misfortune will become its courage; it will make of its endless rejection by colonialism, the absolute rejection of colonization. The secret of the proletariat, Marx once said, is that it bears within it the destruction of bourgeois society. We must be grateful to Memmi for reminding us that the colonized likewise has his secret, and that we are witnessing the infamous death-struggle of colonialism.

A NEW APPROACH TO THE PHILOSOPHY
OF HISTORY: SEARCH FOR A METHOD

. . . Thus the comprehension of existence is presented as the human foundation of Marxist anthropology. Nevertheless, we must beware here of a confusion heavy with consequences. In fact, in the order of Knowledge, what we know concerning the principle or the foundations of a scientific structure, even when it has come—as is ordinarily the case— later than the empirical determinations, is set forth first; and one deduces from it the determinations of Knowledge in the same way that one constructs a building after having secured its foundations. But this is because the foundation is itself a knowing; and if one can deduce from it certain propositions already guaranteed by experience, this is because one has induced it in terms of them as the most general hypothesis. In contrast, the foundation of Marxism, as a historical, structural anthropology, is man himself inasmuch as human existence and the comprehension of the human are inseparable. Historically Marxist Knowledge produces its foundation at a certain moment of its development, and this foundation is presented in a disguised form. It does not appear as the practical foundations of the theory, but as that which, on principle, pushes forward all theoretical knowing. Thus the singularity of existence is presented in Kierkegaard as that which on principle is kept outside the Hegelian system (that is, outside total Knowledge), as that which can in no way be *thought* but only *lived* in the act of faith. The dialectical procedure to reintegrate existence (which is never *known*) as a foundation at the heart of Knowledge could not be attempted then, since neither of the current attitudes—an idealist Knowledge, a spiritual existence—could lay claim to concrete actualization. These two terms outlined abstractly the future contradiction. And the development of anthropological knowing could not lead then to the synthesis of these formal positions: the movement of ideas—as the movement of society—had first to produce Marxism as the only possible form of a really concrete Knowledge. And . . . Marx's own Marxism, while indicating the dialectical opposition between knowing and being, contained implicitly the demand for an existential foundation for the theory. Furthermore, in order for notions like reification and alienation to assume their full meaning, it would have been necessary for the questioner and the questioned to be made one. What must be the nature of human relations in order for these relations to be capable of appearing in certain definite societies as the relations of things to each other? If the reification of human relations is possible, it is because these relations, even if reified, are fundamentally distinct from the relations of things. What kind of practical organism is this which reproduces its life by its work so that its work and ultimately its very reality are alienated; that is, so that they, *as others,* turn back upon him and determine him? But before Marxism, itself a product of the social conflict, could turn to these problems, it had to assume fully its role as a practical philosophy—that is, as a theory clarifying social and political *praxis.* The result is a profound *lack* within contemporary Marxism; the use of the notions mentioned earlier—and many others—refers to a comprehension of human reality which is missing. And this lack is not—as some Marxists declare today—a localized void, a hole in the construction of Knowledge. It is inapprehensible and yet everywhere present; it is a general anemia.

Doubtless this *practical anemia* becomes an anemia in the Marxist man—that is, in us, men of the twentieth century, inasmuch as the unsurpassable framework of Knowledge is Marxism; and inasmuch as this Marxism clarifies our individual and collective *praxis,* it therefore determines us in our existence. About 1949 numerous posters covered the walls in Warsaw: "Tuberculosis slows down production." They were put there as the result of some decision on the part of the government, and this decision originated in a very good intention. But their content shows more clearly than anything else the extent to which man has been eliminated from an anthropology which wants to be pure knowledge. Tuberculosis is an object of a practical Knowledge: the physician learns to know it in order to cure it; the Party determines its importance in Poland by statistics. Other mathematical calculations connecting these with production statistics (quantitative variations in production for each industrial group in proportion to the number of cases of tuberculosis) will suffice to obtain a law of the type $y = f(x)$, in which tuberculosis plays the role of independent variable. But this law, the same one which could be read on the propaganda posters, reveals a new and double alienation by totally eliminating the tubercular man, by refusing to him even the elementary role of *mediator* between the disease and the number of manufactured products. In a socialist society, at a certain moment in its development, the worker is alienated from his production; in the theoretical-practical order the human foundation of anthropology is submerged in Knowledge.

It is precisely this expulsion of man, his exclusion from Marxist Knowledge, which resulted in the renascence of existentialist thought outside the historical totalization of

Knowledge. Human science is frozen in the non-human, and human-reality seeks to understand itself outside of science. But this time the opposition comes from those who directly demand their synthetic transcendence. Marxism will degenerate into a non-human anthropology if it does not reintegrate man into itself as its foundation. But this comprehension, which is nothing other than existence itself, is disclosed at the same time by the historical movement of Marxism, by the concepts which indirectly clarify it (alienation, etc.), and by the new alienations which give birth to the contradictions of socialist society and which reveal to it its abandonment; that is, the incommensurability of existence and practical Knowledge. The movement can *think* itself only in Marxist terms and can *comprehend* itself only as an alienated existence, as a human-reality made into a thing. The moment which will surpass this opposition must reintegrate comprehension into Knowledge as its non-theoretical foundation.

In other words, the foundation of anthropology is man himself, not as the object of practical Knowledge, but as a practical organism producing Knowledge as a moment of its *praxis*. And the reintegration of man as a concrete existence into the core of anthropology, as its constant support, appears necessarily as a stage in the process of philosophy's "becoming-the-world." In this sense the foundation of anthropology cannot precede it (neither historically nor logically). If *existence,* in its free comprehension of itself, preceded the awareness of alienation or of exploitation, it would be necessary to suppose that the free development of the practical organism historically preceded its present fall and captivity. (And if this were established, the historical precedence would scarcely advance us in our comprehension, since the retrospective study of vanished societies is made today with the enlightenment furnished by techniques for reconstruction and by means of the alienations which en-chain us.) Or, if one insisted on a logical priority, it would be necessary to suppose that the freedom of the project could be recovered in its full reality *underneath* the aliena-tions of our society and that one could move dialectically from the concrete existence which understands its freedom to the various alterations which distort it in present society. This hypothesis is absurd. To be sure, man can be enslaved only if he is free. But for the historical man who *knows* himself and *comprehends* himself, this practical freedom is grasped only as the permanent, concrete condition of his servitude; that is, across that servitude and by means of it as that which makes it possible, as its foundation. Thus Marxist Knowledge bears on the alienated man; but if it doesn't want to make a fetish of its knowing and to dissolve man in the process of knowing his alienations, then it is not enough to describe the working of capital or the system of colonization. It is necessary that the questioner understand how the questioned—that is, himself—*exists with his alien-ation,* how he surpasses it and is alienated in this very sur-passing. It is necessary that his very thought should at every instant surpass the intimate contradiction which unites the comprehension of man-as-agent with the knowing of man-as-object and that it forge new concepts, new determinations of Knowledge which emerge from the existential comprehen-sion and which regulate the movement of their contents by its dialectical procedure. Yet this comprehension—as a liv-ing moment of the practical organism—can take place only within a concrete situation, insofar as theoretical Knowledge illuminates and interprets this situation.

Thus the autonomy of existential studies results neces-sarily from the negative qualities of Marxists (and not from Marxism itself). So long as the doctrine does not recognize its anemia, so long as it founds its Knowledge upon a dogmatic metaphysics (a dialectic of Nature) instead of seeking its support in the comprehension of the living man, so long as it rejects as irrational those ideologies which wish, as Marx did, to separate being from Knowledge and, in anthropology, to found the knowing of man on human existence, existentialism will follow its own path of study. This means that it will attempt to clarify the givens of Marxist Knowledge by indirect knowing (that is, by words which regressively denote existential structures), and to engender within the framework of Marxism a veritable *comprehensive knowing* which will rediscover man in the social world and which will follow him in his *praxis*—or, if you prefer, in the project which throws him toward the social possibles in terms of a defined situation. Existentialism will appear therefore as a fragment of the system, which has fallen outside of Knowledge. From the day that Marxist thought will have taken on the human dimension (that is, the existential project) as the foundation of anthropological Knowledge, existentialism will no longer have any reason for being. Absorbed, surpassed and conserved by the totalizing movement of philosophy, it will cease to be a particular inquiry and will become the foundation of all inquiry. The comments which we have made in the course of the present essay are directed—to the modest limit of our capabilities—toward hastening the moment of that dissolution.

Bibliography

I. WORKS BY SARTRE

A. Philosophy

1936. *L'Imagination* (Presses Universitaires). *Imagination* (University of Michigan, 1962).

1937. "La transcendance de l'Ego," *Recherches Philosophiques* VI (1936-1937). *Transcendence of the Ego* (Noonday, 1957).

1939. *Esquisse d'une théorie des émotions* (Hermann). *The Emotions, Outline of a Theory* (Philosophical Library, 1948).

1940. *L'Imaginaire, psychologie phénoménologique de l'imagination* (Gallimard). *Psychology of Imagination* (Philosophical Library, 1948).

1943. *L'Etre et le Néant* (Gallimard). *Being and Nothingness* (Philosophical Library, 1956).

1960. *Critique de la raison dialectique,* I (Gallimard).

B. Fiction

1937. "Le Mur," in *Nouvelle Revue Française* (July). In *The Wall and Other Stories* (New Directions, 1948).

1938. *La Nausée* (Gallimard). *Nausea* (New Directions, 1949).

1939. *Le Mur, suivi de La Chambre, Erostrate, Intimité, L'Enfance d'un Chef* (Gallimard). *The Wall and Other Stories* (New Directions, 1948).

1945-49. *Les Chemins de la liberté* (*Roads to Freedom*). I—*L'Age de raison;* II—*Le Sursis;* III—*La Mort dans l'âme;* IV—*La Dernière chance* (Gallimard). Published by Knopf: *Age of Reason* (1947); *The Reprieve* (1947); *Troubled Sleep* (1951).

C. Drama

1943. *Les Mouches* (Gallimard). In *No Exit and The Flies* (Knopf, 1947).

1944. *Huis-clos* (Gallimard). In *No Exit and The Flies* (Knopf, 1947).

1946. *Morts sans sépulture* (Gallimard). *The Victors,* in *Three Plays* (Knopf, 1949).

1946. *La Putain respectueuse* (Nagel). *The Respectful Prostitute* (Twice A Year Press, 1949).

1947. *Les Jeux sont faits* (Nagel). *The Chips Are Down* (Lear, 1948).

1948. *Les Mains sales* (Gallimard). *Dirty Hands,* in *Three Plays* (Knopf, 1949).

1949. *L'Engrenage* (Nagel). *In the Mesh* (Dakers, 1954).

1951. *Le Diable et le Bon Dieu* (Gallimard). In *The Devil and the Good Lord and Two Other Plays* (Knopf, 1960). Published in England as *Lucifer and the Lord* (Hamilton, 1952).

1954. *Kean* (Gallimard). *Kean,* in *The Devil and the Good Lord and Two Other Plays* (Knopf, 1960).

1955. *Nekrassov* (Gallimard).

1960. *Les Séquestrés d'Altona* (Gallimard). *The Con-demned of Altona* (Knopf, 1961).

D. Essays and Autobiographical Works

1946. *Descartes* (Trait). Introduction and selected texts.
1947. *L'Existentialisme est un humanisme* (Nagel). *Existentialism* (Philosophical Library, 1947).
1947. *Situations* I (Gallimard). Selections in *Literary and Philosophical Essays* (Philosophical Library, 1957).
1947. *Baudelaire* (Gallimard). *Baudelaire* (Horizon, 1949).
1947. *Réflexions sur la question juive,* ed. Paul Morihien (Gallimard). *Anti-Semite and Jew* (Schocken, 1948).
1948. *Situations* II (Gallimard). Contains articles published in *Qu'est-ce que la littérature?*
1948. *Qu'est-ce que la littérature?* (Gallimard). *What Is Literature?* (Philosophical Library, 1949).
1948. *Visages* (Seghers).
1949. *Situations* III (Gallimard). Selections in *Literary and Philosophical Essays* (Philosophical Library, 1957).
1949. *Entretiens sur la politique* [in collaboration with David Rousset and Gérard Rosenthal] (Gallimard).
1952. *Saint-Genêt, cómedien et martyr* (Gallimard). *Saint Genet, Actor and Martyr* (Braziller, 1963).
1953. *L'Affaire Henri Martin* (Gallimard).
1956. *Voies Nouvelles* [in collaboration with J.-J. Mayoux, P. Lescaut, and M. Gauthier] (La Nef de Paris).
1962. *Marxisme et Existentialisme* [in collaboration with Garaudy] (Plon).
1964. *Situations* IV: *Portraits;* V: *Colonialisme et Néo-colonialisme;* VI: *Problèmes du Marxisme* 1; VII:

Problèmes du Marxisme 2 (Gallimard). Selections from IV in *Situations* (Braziller, 1965).

1965. *The Philosophy of Existentialism* [edited by Wade Baskin] (Philosophical Library).

1965. *The Philosophy of Jean-Paul Sartre* [edited by Robert Denoon Cumming] (Random House).

II. SIGNIFICANT ARTICLES BY SARTRE

Most of the articles published by Sartre in *N.R.F.* (1938-1949), in *Cahiers du Sud* (1943-1944), in *Europe* (1939), in *Poésie 44* (1944), in *Figaro* (1945), and in *Les Temps Modernes* beginning in 1946, have been republished in *Situations* I-V. Below are listed only those that have not been republished.

"L'Ange du morbide," *Revue sans titre* (1923).

"Légende de la vérité," *Bifur* (1931).

"La Structure intentionnelle de l'image," *Revue de Métaphysique et de Morale* (September, 1938).

"Discussion sur le péché," *Dieu Vivant* IV.

"Introduction aux Ecrits intimes de Baudelaire," *Confluences* (January-February, 1945).

"Présence noire," *Présence Africaine* (Paris-Dakar, November-December, 1947).

"Les jours de notre vie" [in collaboration with Merleau-Ponty], *Les Temps Modernes* (January, 1950).

"Gide vivant," *Les Temps Modernes* (March, 1952).

"Sommes-nous en démocracie?" *Les Temps Modernes* (April, 1952).

"Les communistes et la paix," *Les Temps Modernes*: I(July, 1952); II (October-November, 1952): III (August 1954).

"Réponse à Claude Lefort [on Marxism]," *Les Temps Modernes* (April, 1953).

"Le colonialisme est un système," *Les Temps Modernes* (March-April, 1956).

"Sur les événements de Hongrie," *L'Exprès* (9 November 1956).

"Le fantóme de Staline," *Les Temps Modernes* (January 1957).

"Vous êtes formidables," *Les Temps Modernes* (May 1957).

"Questions de méthode," *Les Temps Modernes* XIII (1957). *Search for a Method* (Knopf, 1963).

"Nous sommes tous des assassins," *Les Temps Modernes* (March, 1958).

"The Making of a Writer: The Author as Hero, Martyr, and Saint," *Harpers* CCXXIX (September, 1964).

III. WORKS DEVOTED TO THE WRITINGS OF JEAN-PAUL SARTRE

Robert Campbell. *Jean-Paul Sartre ou une littérature philosophique* (Editions Pierre Ardent, 1945).

D. Troisfontaines. *Le Choix de J.-P. Sartre* (Aubier, 1945).

Pierre Boutang and Jean Pingaud. *Sartre est-il un possédé?* (La Table Ronde, 1946).

Francis Jeanson. *Le Problème moral et la pensée de Jean-Paul Sartre* (Editions du Myrte, 1947).

Marc Beigbeder. *L'Homme Sartre* (Bordas, 1947).

Jean Kanapa. *L'existentialisme n'est pas un humanisme* (Editions Sociales, 1947).

Simone de Beauvoir. *The Ethics of Ambiguity.* Trans. by Bernard Frechtman (Philosophical Library, 1948).

Jean-Marie Grévillot. *Les Grands Courants de la pensée contemporaine* (Beauchesne, 1948).

Gilbert Varet. *L'ontologie de Sartre* (Presses Universitaires, 1948).

P.-H. Simon, *L'homme en procès* (Neuchâtel: La Baconnière, 1950).

Régis Jolivet. *Le problème de la mort chez Heidegger et chez Sartre* (Ed. de Fontenelle, 1950).

Pierre de Boisdeffre. *Métamorphoses de la littérature* (Editions Alsatia, 1951) II, pp. 209-307.

Iris Murdoch. *Sartre: Romantic Rationalist* (Yale University Press, 1953).

Pierre de Boisdeffre. *Des Vivants et des Morts* (Editions Universitaires, 1954).

Charles Moeller. *Littérature du XXe siècle* (Albin Michel, 1955).

Cahiers de la Compagnie Madeleine-Jean-Louis Barrault XIII. *Connaissance de Sartre* (Julliard, 1955).

Francis Jeanson. *Sartre par lui-même* (Editions du Seuil, 1956).

Robert Champigny. *Stages on Sartre's Way* (Indiana University Press, 1959).

John D. Wild. *The Challenge of Existentialism* (Indiana University Press, 1959).

Wilfrid Desan. *The Tragic Finale: An Essay on the Philosophy of Jean-Paul Sartre* (Harvard University Press, 1960).

Justus Streller. *Jean-Paul Sartre: To Freedom Condemned.* Trans. Wade Baskin (Philosophical Library, 1960).

René Marill Albérès. *Jean-Paul Sartre: Philosopher Without .Faith.* Trans. Wade Baskin (Philosophical Library, 1961).

Frederic Jameson. *Sartre: The Origins of a Style* (Yale University Press, 1961).

E. G. Kern (ed.). *Sartre, A Collection of Critical Essays* (Prentice-Hall, 1962).

Jacques Salvan. *To Be or Not To Be* (Wayne State University Press, 1962).

M. W. Cranston. *Jean-Paul Sartre* (University of Michigan Press, 1963).

Ronald Davis Laing and D. G. Cooper. *Reason and Violence: A Decade of Sartre's Philosophy, 1950-1960* (Tavistock Publications, 1964).

Adam Schaff. *Marx oder Sartre? Versuch einer Philosophie des Menschen.* Trans. from Polish by Erna Reifer (Europa Verlag, 1964).

Warnock, M. *The Philosophy of Sartre* (Hillary House, 1965).

IV. SIGNIFICANT ARTICLES ON THE WRITINGS OF JEAN-PAUL SARTRE

(Only a few of the important articles are listed.)

Marcel Arland. "Compte rendu de la Nausée," *N.R.F.* (July 1938).

Maurice Merleau-Ponty. "Compte rendu des Mouches," *Confluences* XXV (September-October, 1943).

Gaëtan Picon. "Jean-Paul Sartre et le roman contemporain," *Confluences VIII* (October, 1945).

Maurice Blanchot. "Les Romans de Sartre," *L'Arche* X (October, 1945).

Gabriel Marcel. "Les Chemins de la liberté," *La Nef* XIII (December, 1945).

Jean-José Marchand. "Sartre et les Temps Modernes," *Le Magasin du Spectacle* I (April, 1946).

Claude Cuénot. "Littérature et philosophie chez J.-P. Sartre," *Renaissances* XXI (May, 1946).

Raymond Polin. "Introduction à la philosophie de J.-P. Sartre," *Revue de Paris* XLV (1946).

Claude Roy. "Descriptions critiques," *Poésie* XXXVII (1947).

Georges Blin. "Jean-Paul Sartre et Baudelaire," *Fontaine* LIX (1947).

Yale French Studies. I:1 (1948).

Thierry Maulnier. "Jean-Paul Sartre et le suicide de la littérature," *La Table Ronde* II (February, 1948).

André Blanchet. "Comment Jean-Paul Sartre se représente le Diable et le Bon Dieu," *Etudes* (September, 1951).

Claude Lefort. "Le marxisme et Sartre," *Les Temps Modernes* (April, 1953).

Henri Magnan. "Interview," *Le Monde* (1 July, 1955).

Yale French Studies. *Foray Through Existentialism* XVI (Winter 1955-1956).

Maurice Nadeau. "Sartre et l'affaire Hervé," *Les Lettres Nouvelles* (April, 1956).

Frederic Will. "Sartre and the Question of Character in Literature," *Publications of the Modern Language Association* LXXVI (1961).

Michael Wreszin. "Jean-Paul Sartre: Philosopher as Dramatist," *Tulane Drama Review* V (1961).

Jean-Marie Domenach. "Sartre et l'Europe," *Esprit* IV, V (1961-1962).

Mikel Dufrenne. "La critique de la raison dialectique," *Esprit* IV (1962).

Neal Oxenhandler. "The Metaphor of Metaphor in *La nausée*," *Chicago Review* XV (1952).

Alphonse de Waelhens. "Sartre et la raison dialectique," *Revue philosophie de Louvain* LX (1962).

Madeleine Fields. "De la *Critique de la raison dialectique* aux *Séquestrés d'Altona*," *Publications of the Modern Language Association* LXXVIII (1963).

G. Lichtheim. "Sartre, Marxism, and History," *History and Theory* III (1963).

Raymond Aron. "Jean-Paul Sartre et le marxisme," *Figaro Littéraire* (October-November, 1963).

Dennis Keene. "Engagement," *Essays in Criticism* XIV (1964).

Jean Pellegrin. "L'objet à deux faces dans *La nausée*," *Revue des Sciences Humaines* CXIII (1964).